E

BAR

Brian McFadden

Kohner, Madison & Danforth

ISBN-13 978-0-9992266-5-0

“A Perfect mix of Wholesome Sensuality”

Acknowledgments

I owe my deepest gratitude to so many people for making this book possible. I wish to offer my sincere thanks to Debbie Evans, Barbara's close friend, confidant and business manager. I hope Debbie's love for Barbara shines through. I am especially indebted to the late Raymond Burr, who took the time to speak with me years ago on a wide range of topics, including his close relationship with Barbara. I deeply appreciate the invaluable help of Elaine Quell who located Barb and Bill's house for me, Pascale Sérac who pinpointed the details on this and so many other matters, Ros Patterson who made some wonderful introductions, Kathleen Knowles for her fine interviewing skills, and *Perry Mason* researcher Babs Chicoine, a great detective.

I also wish to thank "Big Dave" Brockman at the wonderful Barbara Hale Annex and some long-time *Perry Mason* friends, including Cecilia Cipriani, Gail Melting, Mary Manuilidu, Heidi Heinecke, Joan Norton and Brigitte Maroillat, who was inspired to become a lawyer by watching *Perry Mason*. For their continued support, my sincere thanks to Sherri Dudman Bauer, Tamarra Green Lee, Constance Bélanger, Sandy Kovar, Andrew Rubenstein, Beth Weiner Lipson, Lauren Cates Fox, and Lynn Hathaway

I am delighted that, once again, Veronica Espinoza Paul has provided the front cover art for this book and my sincere thanks to Sonia Hill for the back cover images.

And, as ever, for her constant love, encouragement and support, I am deeply indebted to my wife (and favorite editor,) Pat!

Table of Contents

INTRODUCTION

For so many of us she will always be the beautiful, talented, resourceful Della Street. She was an independent woman, a model of quiet efficiency, and the perfect partner for *Perry Mason*. But the woman who brought Della to life for millions of television fans was so much more than that.

Don't forget, Barbara was part of Hollywood's 'old school.' We may associate her with the fifties and sixties because of *Perry Mason*, but Barbara first gained fame in the early forties. She was a leading lady at a very young age, the product of a studio system that sought to portray her as part of an all-perfect fantasy world.

The truth was much different. Yes, Barbara's good looks and winning personality opened many doors, but she had to rely on her own strength and determination to follow through on the breaks she got. And, like many of us, Barbara was a study in contradictions.

Barbara was almost universally loved by people in the business, but she could be tough with those who crossed her. She was Hollywood's ideal, wholesome leading lady, but she also liked to flirt. And she almost always projected a calm and serene image, even when dealing with difficult personal problems. But sometimes that serene outer self said more about Barbara the actress than about Barbara the person.

Yes, she was an extraordinary woman, our Barbara, and one whose life story has deserved a book for a very long time. I'd like to think she would be pleased with this one.

LOOKING BACK

They always said she had an angel on her shoulder, and perhaps they were right. It was certainly true that, more often than not, fate had stepped in to set her on a path that was far better than anything she would have dreamed of on her own. But she knew, better than anyone else, that no matter how much the fan magazines attributed her successful career to luck, it was her own hard work, determination and, yes, ambition, that made the difference.

On this day, as she looked back over her life, she remembered the real Barbara Hale, the little girl who wanted to excel in everything she did.

Barbara at Three

And Barbara had excelled. She had been blessed with good looks, extraordinary talent and a drive to succeed. She'd also been blessed with a long life and, surveying it now, she realized she was most grateful for the people she loved. Her children, of course, and also her husband, actor Bill Williams, even though their relationship was often stormy. Despite that, she liked to call him "Daddy Bill." Truth be told, though, some of her fondest memories involved Raymond Burr and the cast and crew of *Perry Mason*. She looked back on those years as some of the best of her life, even though she was working almost non-stop.

How she loved Raymond and how she wished he was still here. But, even as she thought of her *Perry Mason* partner and all the people she loved so much, there was the bittersweet realization that so many of them had "Gone to Europe." That was Barbara's euphemism for passing on. It was so common in the household that even her estate planner had begun saying "When Barbara goes to Europe!"

Funny, but she didn't feel old enough to be getting ready for a grand exit, even though her "grand entrance" had been more than ninety years ago! And what an entrance it was.

Parents always fawn over the baby in the family, but when that baby arrives some nine *years* after her older sister...well let's just say Barbara was the apple of everybody's eye. That included big sister Juanita!

Juanita 9 years old, Barbara 8 months

Barbara was born in DeKalb, Illinois, where the above picture was taken. Juanita was born in the very small town of

Willisburg, Kentucky, where the Hales lived until shortly before Barbara's birth. Most little girls had dolls to play with, but Juanita had a little living doll to pamper and adore.

Things didn't change much after the family moved from DeKalb to Rockford, Illinois. Juanita continued to function as a second mom to the latest little Hale. That's Juanita below, with Barbara warm and snug in a heavy coat and woolen cap, as she smiles and clutches a book!

At this point Barbara was all of four years old and a pretty confident young lady. Being loved will do that to you. It would seem that, in addition to a warm and attentive sister, Barbara had two parents who were willing to sacrifice for the family. Her dad, Luther "Ezra" Hale, apparently moved to DeKalb to make a better go of farming. He then moved to Rockford where he worked to build a landscaping business. But, during the depression when times were tough, he took a temporary job as a laborer in a milling machine factory. In short, he did whatever he had to do to support his family and he eventually became quite successful.

Just as Barbara provided older sister Juanita with a "living doll" to play with, Juanita was able to return the favor as she grew up and had children of her own. Instead of having to sit stuffed bunnies in baby chairs and play "let's pretend" tea party, 11-year-old Barbara had the real thing in baby niece Diana and nephew James.

I love the above picture, because young Barbara looks so happy with her little playmates. I think of it every time I see an episode of Perry Mason where the lovely adult Barbara is serving coffee to her grown-up friends. I can't help thinking of all the practice Barbara had playing a make-believe mom.

The only difference is, instead of serving her big sister's children, she's entertaining Raymond Burr and Bill Hopper.

Barbara had dreams like any little girl. They were the usual ones, nothing all that unrealistic. The future Della Street, like so many children in America, took ballet and tap dancing lessons as a child. Had her home studio, RKO, ever decided to pair her with Fred Astaire, she would have been ready. But RKO, and later Columbia, saw Barbara as more of a wholesome romantic lead, an image she projected because it was part of her real life.

The love Barbara received as a child gave her a special kind of self-confidence infused with an attractive acceptance of others. It was evident even when she was a child. A fifth grade picture at her Rockford grammar school shows

Barbara, front row center, sporting Shirley Temple-type curls.

The other kids liked Barbara and Barbara liked them. And that would carry over into adulthood. Barbara made friends easily wherever she went.

By the time she got to High School, Barbara's popularity was even more evident. She did well in her studies, but managed to find time for extracurricular activities and hanging out with friends. She had always been interested in drawing and began to think seriously about going to art school. To help save the necessary money, she took after-school jobs babysitting, working at a soda fountain and being a store cashier.

But this was one lovely young lady who had plenty of energy, and she also always found plenty of time to play.

Barbara was no shrinking violet when it came to social activities. She especially enjoyed the celebrations after High School football victories! Barbara said she and her friends would drive to a housing subdivision that was being put up at the time.

"The houses weren't there (yet), but the streets were in," she said. "We'd park our cars pointed in a circle, turn our headlights on, and turn our radios on to the same station. We'd all get out in the street and dance. That was our dance floor."

Barbara also acquired a steady boyfriend. And, like the other couples at school, they enjoyed kissing under the Elm trees that gave Rockford its nickname, "The Forrest City."

Ironically, though, the trees that inspired the "Forest City" label were ravaged by Dutch elm disease in the fifties and sixties. But Barbara and her steady, a young fellow named Cam Perks, never forgot each other. They remained friends for life.

Barbara had only so much time for romance anyway, because she was busy with other pursuits. Her main interest remained art, but she found she was attracted to the theater as well. So the young would-be artist joined the Walter Hampden club at school. Hampden was a stage actor well-known for his interpretations of Shakespeare, hence the title for the drama club. Barbara's popularity with her classmates led to her being chosen Home Room Secretary in Junior Year and Queen of the May when she was a senior!

Barbara and her friends at school

But even Barbara admitted she wasn't always the perfect student. There was that day, for example, when she and several other girls, skipped classes to see crooner Frank Sinatra perform at the Coronado Theater in town. What the other girls, and for that matter Barbara herself, didn't know at the time, was that Barb would be giving Frank his first onscreen kiss in a few years! But that story is for another chapter!

From Sinatra fan, to Sinatra co-star

ARTIST AND MODEL

"Drawing is the hobby of 'Barb,' who has very high aspirations of becoming a successful commercial artist."
— Rockford High School Yearbook, 1940

Since her mom and dad were onboard with Barbara's plans to become an artist, Barbara found herself onboard a train heading for Chicago after graduation. Any concerns her family had were eased by the fact that she'd be staying at the YWCA.

Barbara at the YWCA in Chicago

Barbara proved popular with other students at the Art Institute in Chicago, and not just because of her pleasing personality and winning disposition. Her classmates soon discovered that the young girl with the winning smile and lovely figure was the perfect model for their art assignments.

Professors took notice too. One of Barbara's teachers was Roy Ketcham, who had created a comic strip called *Ramblin' Bill,* and he realized that Barbara would be a perfect model for the strip. It couldn't have worked out better for Barbara, giving her some extra money for her stay in Chicago.

And Barbara's modeling opportunities were about to increase substantially, thanks to a lucky break that would eventually lead her to Hollywood!

Barbara's story has been told and retold so many times that it's sometimes difficult to determine fact from myth. This is especially true when trying to sift through studio publicity material and movie magazine articles. The official version of Barbara's entry into the world of big time modeling contends Barbara and another girl were standing on a Chicago street corner, when the owners of a modeling agency drove by. They had just enough time between lights to hand Barbara a business card and ask her to call.

Barbara didn't know the agency owners and viewed it as a joke. The agency owners didn't know Barbara and could only identify her as "The girl in the red coat." According to this version, another friend of Barbara's just happened to be sitting at a lunch counter some time later, next to a lady who just happened to be one of the agency's owners. She also just happened to be talking about the search for the girl in the red coat. The friend spread the word, Barbara got the job and everybody lived happily ever after. Just substitute "Glass Slipper" for "Red Coat" and you've got *Cinderella*!

The funny thing is, the story could well be true. Fate always had a way of stepping in and opening doors for Barbara. And, in this case, the doors led to "The Connie and Al Seaman Models Bureau." It was a well-respected agency and had many top accounts.

Both a talented artist and a lovely model

Barbara was perfect for fashion modeling. She had the ability to project a natural, appealing, freshness that the camera loved.

Barbara's popularity with photographers and clients grew and Connie and Al Seaman knew they had made the right decision in hiring her. The Seaman's were, by all accounts, a couple who tried to help the young people on their roster and Barbara's winning personality led them to offer her a place to stay at their home. The couple also told

Barbara that she would probably have a much brighter future being the person who was *being* drawn rather than the person who was *doing* the drawing.

Barbara had learned at the Chicago Institute that there was a great deal of competition in commercial art. So now, she began to think that modeling might be her true calling. She was getting more assignments for big, brand name products and working for top commercial artists like Gil Elvgren, below.

In addition to her good looks and poise, Barbara had some other real advantages in the modeling business. Although she was only 19 at the time, she could appear more sophisticated and mature in ads where she was dressed in the latest fashions. Posed in a faux classical setting and sporting a sleek little number from Saks Fifth Avenue, Barbara certainly didn't look like a recent high school grad!

Barbara was appearing in major ads for department stores, soft drink companies, automakers and others. And the people who helped make that possible, were now about to play a big role in the next phase of her career.

HEADING FOR HOLLYWOOD

The story of how Barbara Hale transitioned from successful model to aspiring movie star is another one of those tales that has been told over and over again. It first surfaced in movie studio publicity releases of the forties, and was repeated in TV magazines of the fifties and sixties, when *Perry Mason* became popular. Like the saga of Barbara's discovery as a model, it may sound like a publicity tale. But I'm convinced there's no need to begin it with "Long ago and far away."

The basics of the story are simple. Barbara's agent Al Seaman thinks Barbara has what it takes to become a successful actress. He sends pictures of her to a friend at

RKO. The studio likes what it sees, sends a representative to meet with Barbara, pays for her to come to California, and promptly signs her to a contract. It may sound too good to be true, but I believe it because something similar happened to another model who worked for Connie and Al Seaman.

He was a young Chicago native by the name of Jack Moore. As a model, he was quite successful doing newspaper and catalog ads, but he wanted to go to New York to get some acting experience. Al and Connie recommended him to the John Robert Powers Agency in New York, where he earned a living modeling while getting some acting experience under his belt. Then Jack Moore headed for California where, under the name Clayton Moore, he eventually became better known as "The Lone Ranger."

I had the pleasure of meeting Clayton Moore a couple of times over the years and he struck me as a hard-working, friendly person who deserved every success. I'm sure that's the same impression Al and Connie Seaman had of both Clayton Moore *and* Barbara Hale.

So it really isn't a surprise that Al Seaman sent Barbara's pictures to a fellow he had gone to school with who worked at RKO. What *is* a surprise is how quickly things took off from there. The photos wound up on the desk of RKO casting director Ben Piazza. We'll let him pick up the story from there.

"She was a Chicago model when someone sent two photographs of her to my desk. I wrote to Arthur Willy, our New York talent scout, to look her over when he took his next trip to Chicago, (which was very shortly thereafter.) He was favorably impressed, and we signed her."

Piazza helped many starlets, like Peggy Drake, below, sign on the dotted line. But he felt Barbara was special.

“She has great personality, beauty and charm,” said Piazza. He viewed Barbara as a down to earth beauty with star quality. Shortly after signing her, Piazza said, “Barbara Hale has humility...she’s modest and eager to learn.”

Barbara lost no time in getting out to Hollywood after RKO sent the tickets. She hoped for the best, but was realistic about it. She packed light because she felt she might not be staying there all that long. According to one report, she had been dating a serviceman who was now stationed in California, and if all else failed she’d at least get a free trip to see him. At first I doubted the story, until I found out that, in Chicago, Barbara had been living across the street from a group of soldiers who were medical students. It would be very strange indeed, if the guys hadn’t been clamoring for dates with the beautiful young model.

It became apparent that Barbara would be in Hollywood a lot longer than the short time necessary to renew old acquaintances, when she quickly won the approval of RKO chief Charles Koerner. However, Barbara's mother had been understandably leery about her going to Hollywood and had warned her to be careful. So when Koerner told her he wanted her at RKO, she said that she would love to WORK at the studio. About the second or third time Barbara emphasized the word WORK, Koerner just laughed and said, "Well honey, you're going to be safe, don't worry about that, we have a lovely place here called "The Studio Club."

"The Studio Club" was a chaperoned residence for young women in the movie business. It was run by the YWCA and in some ways resembled a sorority house. It was perfect for Barbara and she spent her first year in Hollywood there. For fifteen dollars a week she got lodging plus two meals a day!

Outside Barbara's Studio Club room

Just as there were great publicity stories about *how* Barbara got to Hollywood there were lots of publicity stories about what happened *when* she got there. And, once again, these tales, at least at first glance, sound too good to be true. Complicating matters is the fact that there are slightly different timelines, depending on which version you hear.

The gist of the story is that Barbara barely had time to unpack before she was rushed to the set to replace another actress who was sick. It made for good publicity and quickly spread. The problem is, one version had Barb in front of the cameras in 12 hours, another said 24, and a third claimed 36. It's not that there aren't some kernels of truth in these publicity stories. It's just that the kernels are mixed with so much corn that it's hard to tell the wheat from the chaff!

The corny part here is the "A Star is Born" implication some of the stories carried. The role in question was a very small bit part in the film *Gildersleeve's Bad Day*. It was hardly going to lead to overnight success. However, RKO immediately put out the staged picture below showing Barbara with *Gildersleeve's* star Harold Peary supposedly being photographed for a big press release.

The caption, commenting on how quickly Barbara was cast in her first film, called her "The Windy City Whirlwind!" Again, it was just another example of the very effective RKO publicity machine. But the fact that Barbara was able to do what she was asked to do, on such short notice and with so little experience, says a heck of a lot!

Think about it. She was in high school just a few short years ago, then off to Chicago for art school. Almost immediately her charm and good looks marked her for success in the modeling world, and now she's appearing in her first movie. It's true that fate was kind to Barbara, and she was always the first to admit it. But more importantly, Barbara was always ready when opportunity knocked.

Here's a girl with no motion picture experience, who's told to report to the *Gildersleeve's* soundstage for her first movie. Sure it's a small part, but she doesn't even know what it means to "hit her mark" on the stage floor. Worse yet, she's got to explain to director Gordon Douglas that she's never even worked with a movie script before! Barbara pulls it off and Gordon is impressed. He can't believe she's just arrived at RKO and he congratulates her on a job well done.

If you or I had to do something like that, we'd probably be scared to death, I know I would. Barbara was probably fearful too, but something in her upbringing must have given her an extraordinary amount of confidence. Having a sister like Juanita, who was so much older than Barb and doted on her, may have played a major role.

But it was more than self-confidence that worked in Barbara's favor. Her genuinely pleasing personality was mentioned by almost everyone who came into contact with her at RKO, from studio bigwigs to crewmembers. The fellow who devised the sets for many of Barbara's films was veteran RKO Art Director Al D'Agostino. He said, "She has the one quality that's always in style on the screen: wholesomeness.

With her, it's real. Other girls assume it, but she doesn't put it on. She seems genuine because she *is* genuine."

D'Agostino had plenty of opportunities to get to know Barbara. He worked on all of her early pictures. Like *Gildersleeve's Bad Day*, Barbara's parts in these films were all extremely small but she was learning her trade and they were keeping her extremely busy.

After being rushed into the *Gildersleeve's* picture upon her arrival in February of 1943, she showed up in March in another B-programmer, *The Mexican Spitfire's Blessed Event*. It was, once again, an uncredited role. In April, Barbara was assigned a small role in *The Iron Major*. This was a step up for Barb because it wasn't a B-programmer, and featured a major name, Pat O'Brian. A few weeks later, Barbara once again found herself in a very small role, but in a movie that would become a classic. She appeared in a subway scene in Val Lewton's spooky, *The Seventh Victim*.

In late May, RKO put Barbara in one of their patriotic musicals, *Around the World* with Kay Kyser and his band. She was one of several RKO starlets who adorned the war-time offering.

Just as Barbara has a prominent place next to Kay Kyser in the above publicity photo, she had a little more screen time in this film. She also had a brief line with Kyser. But it was back to relative anonymity when she shot *Government Girl* in June. She was just one of many young ladies in a hotel lobby.

Then, in July, Barbara showed up in another entry in the *Gildersleeve's* series. This one was called *Gildersleeve on*

Broadway, and Barbara had a small part as a young lady selling hosiery.

It was around this time that Barbara also did a comedy short called, of all things, *Politics and Prunes*! The star was Edgar Kennedy, known for his so-called "slow-burn" going all the way back to the silent days. Hugh Beaumont, who would go on to play Ward Cleaver on *Leave It To Beaver*, also appears in the short. Once again, Barb has a very small part, but she's a standout from her first line, a brief exchange with Kennedy.

Again, the big surprise here, as is the case with her other bit parts, is how radiant and ready Barbara appears to be in this small, supporting role. As they used to say, "She's a knockout!" And perhaps that's why, even though the entire short runs only sixteen minutes, the producers decided to give Barbara more screen time and another line at the end of the segment, when she assures Kennedy she'll let the press know he's available for interviews.

This last brief scene was mostly light-hearted, but in a split second the photographer also captured a wistful look on Barbara's face that would become part and parcel of her appeal. The truth is, even at this early stage of her career, the camera simply loved Barbara!

She had come so far in such a short time. It's hard to believe, but Barbara had been at RKO less than a year. Now one phase of this talented young lady's career was closing and another was about to begin.

HIGHER AND HIGHER

Barbara always referred to her early days at RKO as her "Paid Education," a training ground where she got paid to learn everything she needed to know about the movie business. There were the invaluable informal lessons that she received just by being on the lot. As a former art student and model, said Barb, "It was great to go into the Art Department and watch the men and women work. I was able to go where they built the big statues and columns for the movies and help them...they let me help them work!" And Barbara said she really enjoyed visiting the Wardrobe Department and talking with the head of fashion for woman.

There were plenty of formal lessons as well. In the picture below, Barbara and fellow studio novice Robert Clarke, learn from RKO Acting Coach Lillian Albertson.

Like so many other friends she met at RKO, Robert Clarke was a guest star on *Perry Mason* with Barb years later. But in these early days, RKO just wanted to make sure that its young hopefuls would be ready for whatever came along. In addition to drama, Barbara took singing and dancing lessons and they were about to come in *very* handy!

Frank Sinatra was a hot property when Barbara and her friends had gone to see him back in Rockford. By 1943 he was a full-fledged idol! The movie studios wanted him and he'd made cameo musical appearances in a few films, but it was RKO who signed him for his first feature.

The studio purchased the rights to a Broadway play called *Higher and Higher*. The musical comedy, which starred Jack Haley, had a complicated plot but a good score by Rodgers and Hart. Yet, in an unusual move, RKO decided to dump most of the original score and replace it with songs by Jimmy McHugh and Harold Adamson, two men who frequently had pop hits with songs composed for movies,

That was the first hint that the RKO version of *Higher and Higher* was going to be special. The second was all the publicity RKO was busy generating about the film in the summer of 1943. Fans learned Jack Haley, from the theater version, would repeat his Broadway role. (This was by contractual obligation.) Meanwhile, French actress Michéle Morgan would be the female lead. And, although he wouldn't be the star, the really big news was that Frank Sinatra would play a featured role and sing several songs.

According to those early press releases, Sinatra's love interest in the film would be Constance Moore, which seemed to make sense since Moore had begun her career as a singer and this movie was a musical. But something changed between the announcement and the start of filming in July. There could be several factors. Some may have felt Moore was too sophisticated-looking for the role. She was slightly older than Barbara and lacked her innocent appearance. Meanwhile, Barbara had the advantage of being friends with almost everybody on the film, including Producer/Director Tim Whelan.

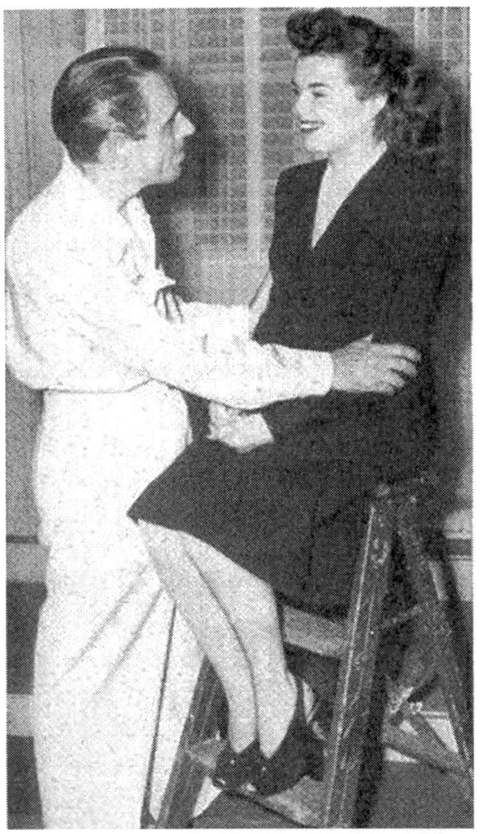

Barbara with Director Tim Whelan

But the biggest factor in casting Barbara as Sinatra's love interest was probably the publicity it generated. It was hard to beat the true story of a high school girl who skipped class to see a young teenage idol in the making, and then wound up starring opposite him on the silver screen a few years later.

This was the kind of story the public relations people at RKO simply couldn't resist. The hype started the minute it was announced that Barbara had been chosen for the part. The first PR release had a picture of Barbara jumping for joy, supposedly taken the moment she got the good news!

The jumping picture may have been staged, but Barbara's joy was real. She had good reason to celebrate. Barbara wasn't the star of the film...far from it. She was listed pretty far down in the credits. But that didn't in any way reflect the impact she had on the audience, especially young Sinatra fans.

In fact, the credits were rather misleading. The nominal star was Jack Haley, best remembered for his role as "The Tin Man" in *The Wizard of Oz.* But Haley was 46 at the time this movie was filmed and hardly a dashing leading man.

That was fine, though, since the whole movie was really designed as a framework to introduce Frank Sinatra. And it provided Barbara with her most visible role to date.

As a high society beauty, Barbara gets to sing with Sinatra and, by the time the film ends, she's engaged to him. Needless to say, the fan magazines and gossip columns were filled with this "Cinderella" story of a real-life bobbysoxer who gets to be romanced by her idol on screen.

Everybody was asking Barbara about what it was like to work with Sinatra, and most of her responses at the time, were like this one: "I saw Frank Sinatra five years ago, before he was famous. I was crazy about his singing. Working with him was my biggest thrill out here to date. Frank is very sweet." Years later, when interviewed while appearing on Perry Mason, Barbara said she had a case of the jitters when she first met Sinatra, but "he's been a dear friend ever since."

If Barbara didn't want to talk too much about her relationship with Frank, it seemed everyone else did! Magazines may not have known anything, but that didn't stop them from making up provocative headlines.

The film was a definite plus for Barbara, but after sampling the rarified atmosphere of a big-budget musical, she had to come back down to earth. Barbara had one more film to make for RKO before the end of the year. It was a programmer, but at least Barbara had a decent role.

The Falcon was a successful B-mystery series for RKO that had begun with George Sanders playing the lead. When Sanders got tired of the role, he was replaced by his real-life brother Tom Conway. By the time Barbara came along, Conway had already appeared in four of the films and the studio was varying locations to maintain interest. This time around RKO sent the detective "Out West," supposedly to Texas. However, the farthest Tom Conway and Barbara actually got was the Corriganville movie ranch in Simi Valley, California.

The film did good business, with the New York Times calling it a "Whodunit with Western atmosphere," saying, "Tom Conway is still the dapper Falcon," and mentioning Barbara Hale as among the "girls in the case." The movie wrapped in early November of 1943. Barb had been working virtually non-stop since she arrived in Hollywood the previous February. The crazy schedule had been a blessing in one sense. It kept her from dwelling too much on just how homesick she was.

Every now and then, Barbara would slip when talking to the press, and say how much she missed her "kids" back home. She'd have to explain that, just as Juanita had helped raise her, she was helping to raise Juanita's two children, Jimmy and Diana Lee. Finally, now that the year was almost over, she'd be able to go home and visit with the family. Bing Crosby had just recorded a new song called "I'll Be Home for Christmas," and it was climbing up the charts as Barbara headed back to Rockford, Illinois for a joyful holiday reunion!

HOMECOMING QUEEN

Santa was as popular as ever in 1943, but in Rockford, Illinois that year, he had to share the headlines with someone else. Word that Barbara Hale was coming home for the first time since heading to Hollywood spread like wildfire! It was mid-December and her nephew Jimmy was in the Christmas program at P.R. Walker school. Barbara couldn't wait to get over to her old grade school to watch the show and meet with Jimmy, (below left.)

If there had been buttons on Jimmy's sweater they'd definitely be popping off! But he wasn't the only one to be proud of his aunt. The whole town was busy celebrating!

All of the kids at the school were star struck. Barbara spent an hour-and-a-half signing autographs after her nephew's play. Back then, and for the rest of her life, Barbara was happy to do it. She figured it went with the territory. And there was also a little something extra: Barbara Hale genuinely liked people!

Of course, Barbara was also enjoying the opportunity to spend time catching up with her mom and dad, as this old press clipping indicates.

A Pretty Starlet Comes Home

Everybody had questions for Barbara. What was Hollywood like? Barbara said it was a lot like any other town and it would be just fine if she didn't miss her family so much. And when asked what heartthrob Frank Sinatra was like, she said he was nice, he was cooperative, and she liked the excitement of working with him because it took her mind off her homesickness and helped her fight the urge to "take the next train back home." Looking at an unretouched photo of Barb and Frank, it's obvious that she was still really a kid under all the sophistication, and it was only natural to miss her family.

Barbara told her friends in Rockford that another way she kept busy was by getting involved in projects to help servicemen. She said she'd go to the Hollywood Canteen, visit men who were confined to hospitals, and even act as a tour guide for soldiers and sailors who wanted to see RKO Studios.

Barbara continued that commitment while she was home. She visited the parents of school friends who were now in the service, and appeared wherever she felt she could be of help. Barbara donned a Red Cross uniform to help with a fundraiser for the organization, and showed up in civilian garb at Rockford's Coronado Theater to help sell War Bonds.

Officials were so pleased by the way Barbara's presence boosted bond sales, that they persuaded RKO to extend her stay. However, all good things eventually come to an end.

BACK TO *REEL* LIFE!

After being treated like a super-star in Rockford, it must have been quite a change for Barbara to return to RKO. Luckily, Barbara never took herself too seriously, so finding out that her next picture was a programmer based on the *Fibber McGee and Molly* radio series didn't seem to bother her. In the film, called *Heavenly Days*, Barbara and Gordon Oliver (below) play reporters.

While Oliver wasn't especially well known as an actor, he went on to become a successful producer of such popular TV shows as *Mr. Lucky*, *Peter Gunn*, and *It Takes a Thief.*

People often wonder how Barbara seemed to know almost everybody in the business in later years. The answer is simple: She worked with almost everybody in the business in her early years!

For whatever reason, RKO seemed to like the idea of casting Barbara in film versions of popular radio shows. She'd already appeared in two *Gildersleeves* and a *Fibber McGee and Molly*. Now, RKO's next assignment for Barbara was yet another radio spinoff.

The radio characters "Lum" and "Abner" were created by Chester Lauck and Norris Goff. As the owners of a rural store, they were constantly getting into trouble with their money making schemes. RKO began making movies based on the show in 1940 and *Goin' to Town*, which began filming in April of 1944, was the fifth in the series. Barbara looks great in publicity pictures with Lauck and Goff that show them in full makeup.

But RKO could never resist the temptation to get a little extra publicity by including some glamour shots in its press packages. Not content to show a lovely, conservatively dressed Barbara with a couple of old codgers, they had Lauck and Goff remove their "Lum and Abner" makeup, and pose for some romantic photos with their beautiful co-star!

You can't blame the studio for constantly snapping shots of Barbara. Everyone knew she was unusually attractive and they wanted to make the most of it. Her films were still in the B category, but she was getting noticed.

Like other studios, RKO pushed for pinup pictures and Barbara posed for her fair share. Cheesecake was common at the time, and Barbara was already familiar with it. Gil Elvgren, who had worked with Barbara on national advertising accounts back in Chicago, was also one of the most prolific pinup producers of the day and Donna Reed, Arlene Dahl and Kim Novak were among his other models.

The famous female pinup artist Pearl Frush thought Barbara perfect for pinups too. Pinups at the time were quite tame by today's standards. In general, they depicted lovely young woman with wholesome faces in slightly risqué costumes. Barbara's face practically screamed "Wholesome," even in pinups!

The studio, of course, wanted the same kind of "leg-art" displayed in pinup pictures, so it could attract attention to Barbara's movies. The best way to do so was to combine a sexy picture with a manufactured "story" that the newspapers might pick up. So, even though you know and I know that there was never any real need for Barbara to mount a camera boom at the studio, the publicity folks released the following picture.

After all, who are we to say that a lovely young woman in a skimpy costume aboard a camera rig isn't a major news story? Such was the life of a movie starlet in the forties!

For her next movie, RKO decided to reteam Barbara with Tom Conway in *The Falcon in Hollywood*. The film had a good gimmick in that most of it took place inside a movie studio, and if you want to get a look at what the RKO lot looked like in Barbara's day, this is the perfect opportunity. Meanwhile, Barbara and Tom make quite the dapper pair decked out in the latest 1944 fashions.

The Falcon in Hollywood was one of the more successful entries in the series, turning a substantial profit. Barbara liked Conway and, many years later when an alcohol problem had gotten the best of him, she would join *Perry Mason* producer Gail Patrick and Raymond Burr in trying to help.

Despite her hectic movie schedule, Barbara somehow managed to maintain a busy social life while at RKO. Around this time, the gossip columns were hinting that she was serious about radio performer Dennis Day. He was a nice guy who worked with Jack Benny for years, usually portraying himself as a nerdy, naïve boy singer. He was actually a few years older than Barbara, but came across as less mature.

At the opposite end of the spectrum, Barbara was dating Hungarian-born director André de Toth, who was nine years her senior. He eventually wound up marrying Veronica Lake, the actress who started the peek-a-boo haircut craze. But Barbara remained friends with de Toth, and years later he directed her in one of her better fifties' films, *Last of the Comanches.*

At this point, it might not be a bad idea to take a look at another young RKO contract player who was drawing the attention of gossip columnists at the time. His name was

Herman August Wilhelm Katt. For some strange reason, studio officials didn't think that name would look very good on a theater marquee, so he was rechristened Bill Williams. The young man was beginning to get better pictures and movie magazines said he was dating Rosemary La Planche.

The former Miss America was also a contract player at RKO, although her stint there didn't last very long. After leaving, she wound up in the poverty row classic, *The Devil Bat's Daughter*.

Of course, Bill Williams didn't know at the time that his former girlfriend would eventually morph into *The Devil Bat's Daughter*. But he was also unaware that he'd soon be meeting an angel, and his days of playing the field were about to come to an end.

BOY MEETS GIRL ON THE STUDIO LOT

There are so many versions of how Barbara Hale and Bill Williams got together, that you might as well just take your pick. One says they met while taking acting classes at RKO, and there's a lot of evidence to back that up. The picture below shows RKO acting tutor Lillian Albertson, (Right, holding script) putting Bill and Barb through their paces.

RKO certainly wasn't a huge studio. Barbara and Bill often passed each other when walking on the lot and would wave 'hello,' and even occasionally have coffee in the commissary, but nothing much more than that. Barbara later admitted the minute she saw the young actor with curly hair she thought, "Hmmmm....very nice," but she couldn't figure out why he was so quiet. Barbara was always quick-thinking, and it didn't take her long to come up with a way to spend a little time with Bill. Barbara had a film coming up called *West of the Pecos* with Bob Mitchum.

She had a hard time getting the female lead in the film because the script called for her to masquerade as a boy at one point, and the producer thought she was too pretty. But once she was signed, she was glad to learn that Edward Killy would be the director. He liked Barbara and had worked with her before when she had a small part in *The Iron Major*.

Part of *West of the Pecos* would be shot on location in Lone Pine, a popular area for producing westerns more than 200 miles away from Hollywood. Barb asked Killy if he could find a part for Bill Williams. He said he could use Bill in a small part on the first day of shooting and then again on the last, which would keep him there for the entire production. "Is that good," said Killy? Barbara says she responded, with a big smile, "Oh Yeah, that's wonderful!"

And it was, because it gave Bill and Barbara their first real chance to get to know each other. Even though she was rooming with Rita Corday in Lone Pine, (they had appeared together in films like *The Falcon in Hollywood* and *Gildersleeve on Broadway* in the past) Barbara and Bill had time to talk, and they were pleasantly surprised by what they learned.

"We were sent to Lone Pine to make *West of the Pecos*," said Bill. "Barbara had the lead. I only had a small part. We took lots of walks and managed to see quite a bit of each other." As they talked, Barbara got an insight into why Bill had been so quiet. He had grown up poor...really poor...in Brooklyn, New York.

"I was a slum kid," said Bill. My father died when I was six years old, and my mother worked like a dog as a waitress to pay a couple to take care of me. You could hardly call it room and board, because I slept in the bathtub, but they were kind to me, and it was home. I can remember, all too vividly, what it was like to be broke, really broke."

Because of his background, it was hard for Bill to trust others. It took him time to decide if a person was genuine. He admitted that he was confused about Barbara in the beginning. Because she was so pretty, he thought she might be spoiled. And, with his trust issues, he thought she was too good to be true. He thought she was overly nice and at first assumed it was a put-on, an act to get ahead in the business. He soon learned that wasn't the case at all.

"For two weeks after our return (from Lone Pine,) we were both busy working. Then, one day on the lot we met, and I asked her for a date. We went out, and I asked for a date for the following week. Then it was one date a week, two, three, and then every night."

Luckily for Barbara, she had moved from the YWCA Studio Club, where there was a strictly enforced curfew. At RKO, Barbara had run into Harold Soldinger, a man she knew from her modeling days in Chicago. He was now a film cutter at the studio. She became close friends with Soldinger and his wife Annette, and they would often invite her over for a home cooked meal, and eventually they invited Barbara to move in with them.

Barb began bringing Bill over to the Soldinger's place and the two couples hit it off. Nobody was exactly rolling in dough at the time, so they'd just entertain themselves after dinner. Often they'd roll up the rug and dance to the record player. Annette began to get work as a stand-in for Barbara, so on days when Harold and the ladies were working at RKO and Bill was free, he'd make dinner and have it ready when they got back.

Meanwhile, fears Bill originally had that the studio would object to a romance involving two contract players proved to be unfounded. In fact, RKO seemed to like the idea. Studio executives were impressed with Bill, and Barbara's stock with the company went up when she and Bob Mitchum made RKO a tidy profit in *West of the Pecos*.

But Barbara had one more B-movie to appear in before her fortunes would really change. It was a war movie called *First Yank into Tokyo*, starring Tom Neal, an ex-college boxer who later caused a scandal by beating up Franchot Tone in a fight over actress Barbara Payton. Still later Neal was convicted of involuntary manslaughter in the death of one of his wives. It's things like this that make you wonder what a nice girl like Barbara Hale was doing in the business!

Sometimes Barbara wondered too, and that's why she was so happy to now have someone she could confide in. She was still very lonely and, at times, felt like running back home to her family in Rockford. Bill was a city boy, but he had the clean-cut look of the guys she used to date in Rockford.

Barbara explained that, when it seemed she was at her lowest, most lonesome and most discouraged, Bill would just happen to come by. And then he'd try to lend a helping hand.

"Somehow, without seeming to," said Barbara, "he'd discover what was the matter. Billy would always know just the right thing to say to help me."

And it worked the other way around too. At one point, Bill actually contemplated getting out of the business. He had a chance to go with one of the airline companies as a navigator. Before he went into the service, he'd been a shuttle pilot for Consolidated Airlines and he liked flying. He asked for Barbara's advice, and she suggested that he give acting a little more time. Not long after, he got his first big role in *Those Endearing Young Charms*. It was the first in a string of more substantial roles for the young actor. RKO said audience response to Bill in *Those Endearing Young Charms* was impressive enough for the studio to give him a bigger role in his next film, *Deadline at Dawn*, (below) with Susan Hayward.

The film noir received mixed reviews and Bill did a good job as a naïve sailor, but it was Hayward's performance that stood out.

In between acting assignments, the studio would send Bill out on promotional tours to plug other people's movies. That became a sore point with Bill, as we shall see later. He wanted to be making movies of his own, not spending time on publicity junkets for films he had nothing to do with. He resented it, even when the film starred Barbara. Below, RKO sends Alan Carney, Jane Greer, Marc Cramer, Nan Leslie, and Bill out on the road to plug Barbara's movie *First Yank into Tokyo*.

The above photo was taken October 8, 1945 in Seattle. A short time later, Bill headed back to Los Angeles to start filming *Til the End of Time*. That same October, Barbara was starting a new film too, called *Lady Luck*. This was a big production for RKO. It starred Robert Young and the studio borrowed Frank Morgan (the Wizard in *The Wizard of Oz*) from MGM, and James Gleason (co-star of the *Hildegarde Withers* mysteries and scores of other films) from Twentieth-

Century Fox. Barbara often looked back fondly on *Lady Luck* as the film that provided her first taste of “full stardom.” The girl from Rockford could hardly believe that her name was right up there with Robert Young’s!

There’s a great story Barbara told about the way her co-stars looked out for her. The director of the film didn’t like Barbara because he had pushed his girlfriend for the role Barbara got. So he gave her a hard time one day when she asked for a few minutes to rehearse a scene. Bob Young said very loudly, “That’s alright, Barbara, someday you’ll get a GOOD director,” and walked off the set. Frank Morgan put his arm around Barbara and said, “I couldn’t agree more with Bob. You’ll have a GOOD director someday.” Then James Gleason joined them and the three refused to come back until the director apologized to Barb!

Morgan, Barb, Young, Gleason (insert)

Bill's movie, *Til the End of Time*, came out in the summer of 1946. The story, about former servicemen trying to readjust to civilian life after the war, was very timely. The film was a success and made a substantial profit for RKO. Bill was quite good in it, but it was his co-stars Guy Madison, Dorothy McGuire, and Robert Mitchum who got most of the attention.

Charles Koerner, The RKO chief who approved Barbara Hale's contract, was following Bill's progress closely. He liked them both, and now that their romance was the subject of so much press coverage, he thought pairing the two in a movie might be a good idea. After all, movie magazines seemed to report on everything the "two kids" did.

The story of two good-looking Hollywood lovebirds who met on a studio lot captured the imagination of the fans. And all of the top gossip columnists of the day were covering the romance. There were items by Walter Winchell, Jimmie Fiddler, and Hedda Hopper.

Barbara and Hedda

This was a good decade before Hedda's son, William Hopper, would appear with Barbara and Raymond Burr on *Perry Mason*, playing private detective Paul Drake!

Like so many Hollywood projects that seem promising, the idea of turning Barbara and Bill into America's next pair of famous screen sweethearts, had to be put on hold. Then, as now, life has a habit of getting in the way!

I'VE GOT A SECRET

As 1946 dawned, Barbara's real life seemed to be following the "Cinderella Story" narrative being circulated by all the fan magazines. The young lady who was studying art in Chicago a few short years ago, had gone from starlet to star at RKO, fans were eagerly following her romance with a handsome young actor, and the studio chief had approved a plan to pair the attractive couple in a new movie.

True, some of the gossip columnists were wondering why it was taking so long for "Babs" and Bill Williams to set a date, but that could be explained away by pre-wedding jitters. What most people didn't know back then, and few are aware of today, was that Bill Williams was *already* married! Bill was young, but he'd led a rather complicated life.

Bill's father died when he was only six years old. His mother had to work long hours to support little William Katt, and paid the upstairs neighbors in her Brooklyn, New York tenement to look after him. Bill remembered, "They had a lot of kids of their own. I was the littlest one in the group, and I remember that for a long time I slept in the bathtub because that was the only place they had to put me."

It was a tough neighborhood and Bill had a hard time, but he developed an interest in sports that proved to be a saving grace! He planned on a career in construction engineering, but he became a junior scholastic swimming champ, which led to offers to take part in various aquatic reviews. An agent spotted him during a performance at the ritzy Sands Point Beach Club in Long Island, New York. Bill was offered a job as a member of an acrobatic dancing act and promptly went on tour.

Somewhere along the way, he found himself in St. Louis, where he got involved with, of all things, the St. Louis Municipal Opera Company. More importantly, he also got involved with a young lady who was already working at the Opera Company named Ruth Morgan. The couple hit it off and decided to wed.

Years later Bill said, "I guess Ruth and I were too young when we were married to know what we wanted from life and from each other. We simply didn't see alike about anything. It was an impossible situation and we separated long before I came into pictures or ever even heard of Barbara."

It is true that Bill and his first wife had been estranged for several years when he finally filed for divorce in the fall of 1945. He said he viewed the divorce as a matter of "finishing up unfinished business."

It's sometimes rather difficult to work out the order of events in Bill's life, because accounts often differ. And there isn't a great deal available on Ruth Morgan. But I did find an article in the May 24th, 1934 edition of the St. Louis Post-Dispatch, indicating she was among those rehearsing for the group's performance of Jerome Kern's "Sweet Adeline."

BALLET AND CHORUS OF MUNICIPAL OPERA

Names of 17 Dancers and 66 Singers Now Rehearsing Announced.

Members of the ballet are Katherine Hanaway, Dorothy Harvey, Sonja Karlow, Rosemary Powell, Evan Ritter, Sally Argo, Audrey Vitt, Ruth Morgan, Arline Wiedman, Lala Baumann, June Smith, Dorothy Pratt, Carole Clyde, Peggy Phillips, Gretchen Kimmel, Thora Roberts ad Sheila Harling.

Ruth is mentioned about halfway down and the date is consistent with Bill's claim that he was too young, only 19, at the time of his first marriage.

The fact remained, though, that Barbara and Bill would have to wait until Bill would be free to marry. And, even after filing, it was several more long months before the divorce was final. That's why it took so long for the couple to feel confident enough to announce their engagement. On April 4, 1946, columnist Jimmie Fiddler was among the first to provide a tentative wedding date. He said Babs and Bill would tie the knot sometime in mid-June.

But, as it turned out, the actual date would be June 22.

Barbara and her family needed a little time to make all the preparations necessary for a traditional wedding at the little stone church in Rockford, which the family had long attended. Barb and Bill wanted to get to Rockford early, because there were so many things to do. That included making sure Barbara's wedding dress was perfect!

Barbara was thrilled to be back home, with her dad (helping mom hem the dress,) and little cousin Linda looking on. Barb was looking forward to having Linda and all of her relatives attend what she hoped would be a nice, small family wedding.

A FAIRY-TALE WEDDING

So much for Barbara's idea of a small, family wedding! Although the church was, and still is, technically in Rockton, a stone's throw from Rockford, It turned out everybody in Rockford *and* Rockton wanted to be on hand to see the two Hollywood stars get hitched.

As one of Barbara's cousins said, the wedding caused "the biggest excitement in Rockford since the coming of the railroad!" The good news is, the crowds stayed outside while the happy couple took their vows. The minister who performed the ceremony, Dr. B.E. Allen, made sure of that. Before the ceremony, Dr. Allen spoke in front of the church, urging everyone to be respectful and give the couple space.

Barbara had known Dr. Allen since she was a little girl.

When he was in the pulpit giving a sermon, she would sit with her family in a pew, sketching his likeness. After services, she'd present him with her efforts and he was always delighted. Barb had lovingly nicknamed Dr. Allen "Pappy." Barbara's dad walked his daughter down the aisle.

Barbara's matron of honor, not surprisingly, was her big sister Juanita, and Barb saw to it that two of her young nieces also had a major role to play. As a little girl, Barbara had dreamed of a big wedding, surrounded by all the people she loved. And she especially wanted children to be there since, being a child herself at the time, she felt kids often got cheated out of being able to do the fun stuff grownups did. So, she asked her nieces to sing a song at the wedding.

After the ceremony, out on the church steps, the perfect couple appeared to be in perfect harmony.

But now look very closely at the picture below.

Once Bill and Barbara got off the church steps and out among the crowds of fans, it appears there was a real difference in attitude between the two newlyweds. We see Barbara enthusiastically greeting fans, while Bill seems to be trying to pull her away.

A dear friend of mine, who was very close to Barbara, told me her feelings toward the fans never changed. If she went out to lunch or dinner with Barb, she was always prepared for her meal to go cold. Because whenever a fan approached the table for an autograph or just to chat, Barbara would always make time for them.

Bill did have reason to try to hurry Barb along on their wedding day. They had the reception to attend at the nearby Wagon Wheel restaurant, where the two newlyweds would cut their cake!

The Wagon Wheel was the most popular restaurant in the area and the perfect place for Barbara and Bill's reception.

It had been built of repurposed wood from rail trestles and posts, giving the place a folksy, down home look, which complimented the family atmosphere of Barbara's wedding. Shortly after the wedding, the owner expanded and the restaurant became the center of a resort. It thrived for decades, until the original owner died in the seventies. It went through several owners and several fires and closed in 1989. In 2004, what was left of the once famous restaurant and resort was demolished.

I hope you will forgive me for the brief diversion on Barbara's wedding reception site. It's just that I couldn't help but go back to that June day when Barbara and Bill enjoyed their wedding cake, and undoubtedly imagined a lifetime of bliss. Meanwhile, their host was contemplating the huge expansion he planned, and dreaming that it would guarantee that his resort would last forever. Life doesn't always cooperate. Not for restaurant owners *or* for newlyweds.

But, in the days and weeks after the wedding, Barbara and Bill had little time to do much long-term thinking. They were too busy! The night of the wedding they headed down to Chicago's famed Palmer House, where they occupied the bridal suite. Next, they headed for a variety of destinations, including those honeymooner favorites New York City and Niagara Falls. If they got bumped from a flight, no problem: they'd just take the train.

It was fun, but sometimes hectic. In New York, for example, they had to put in an appearance at an RKO convention. That was fine, though. The two of them knew how important studio events were to their careers. This was an important time for both of them.

They had finished their first important picture together, *A Likely Story*, in April. This was the film where they were supposed to be billed as "RKO's New Starring Team." But it would take a year for *A Likely Story* to be released.

And when Bill and Barb got back from their honeymoon, they had no way of knowing whether they'd be RKO's "New Starring Couple" because the man who had championed teaming them up, was dead. RKO chief Charles Koerner's death earlier in the year had taken everyone by surprise. When they celebrated his birthday in October of 1943, on the set of *Tender Comrades*, there was no way of knowing it would be among his last. Koerner was only 49 when he died of leukemia in 1946. Shown below: Koerner, Ginger Rogers, Producer David Hempstead, and Director Edward Dmytryk.

It was Ginger Rogers who said there were so many different studio presidents at RKO that she had to check the name on the door to make sure she didn't call the new boss by the old boss's name! Koerner had brought stability, and he was always in Barb and Bill's corner. Now things were changing.

SETTING UP HOUSE

Although Barbara and Bill returned to an unsettled situation at RKO, the task of setting up a new household provided a welcome diversion. When they were dating, publicity articles invariably referred to the home she and Bill were working on as one Barbara had purchased on her own. That wasn't true.

Barbara had gone looking for a home for both of them. After finding one she thought was perfect, she went to Bill to see if they had enough money for the down payment. They didn't, but RKO let Bill borrow against his contract. It really was an adorable little place, and they made it their own.

Barbara had chosen wisely. The six room cottage was on a sixty-by-hundred-forty foot lot in the San Fernando Valley, not far from the home her friends the Soldingers purchased.

One of my favorite pictures of Barb shows her outside the house, leaning on a replica horse-head hitching post.

Like many things inside and outside the house, the hitching post was made by Bill. He was a do-it-yourselfer through and through, loved getting his hands dirty, and couldn't see spending a buck if he could make it himself.

It was just as well that Barbara and her husband had things to do at their new home, because RKO was having a tough time figuring out what to do following the loss of Barb and Bill's mentor Charles Koerner. Amid lots of reshuffling of executive positions, Dore Schary would eventually be put in charge. But he didn't take over until January of 1947.

In the meantime, RKO's stable of actors waited nervously to see what would happen. Barbara was among the lucky ones because *Lady Luck*, which she had shot in late 1945, wasn't released until October of 1946. So RKO kept her in the public eye by having her do publicity for the film. And Bill was pressed into service too, since the studio didn't have a motion picture assignment for him at the time. That's a shame, because Bill wasn't getting the chance to show his versatility. Barbara had that chance and she proved herself up to the task in *Lady Luck*. She's quite sophisticated and sexy in this one, taking Robert Young's "little black book" in stride, accepting his suggestion that she simply tear out the pages and leave with him.

Barbara and Bill dutifully headed out on the promotional tour in October. As mentioned earlier, Bill really didn't like being on the road doing publicity for films he wasn't even in.

He felt, not unreasonably, that his career would be better served by being back at RKO making his *own* films. This would become a real sore point later. However, in this particular case there was some rationale for having Bill accompany Barbara. They were billed in their theater appearances as "Hollywood's Young Honeymooners." This provided some early publicity for another film, *A Likely Story*, which was also already in the can, but wouldn't reach theaters for several more months.

It wasn't the only production that would take several months to arrive. In December, Louella Parsons reported, "Barbara Hale and Bill Williams are expecting the Stork." Sure enough, on July 24, 1947, lovely little Willa Johanna arrived! Named after Barbara's mother Willa, and Bill's mom Johanna, Barb and Bill would eventually call her "Jody."

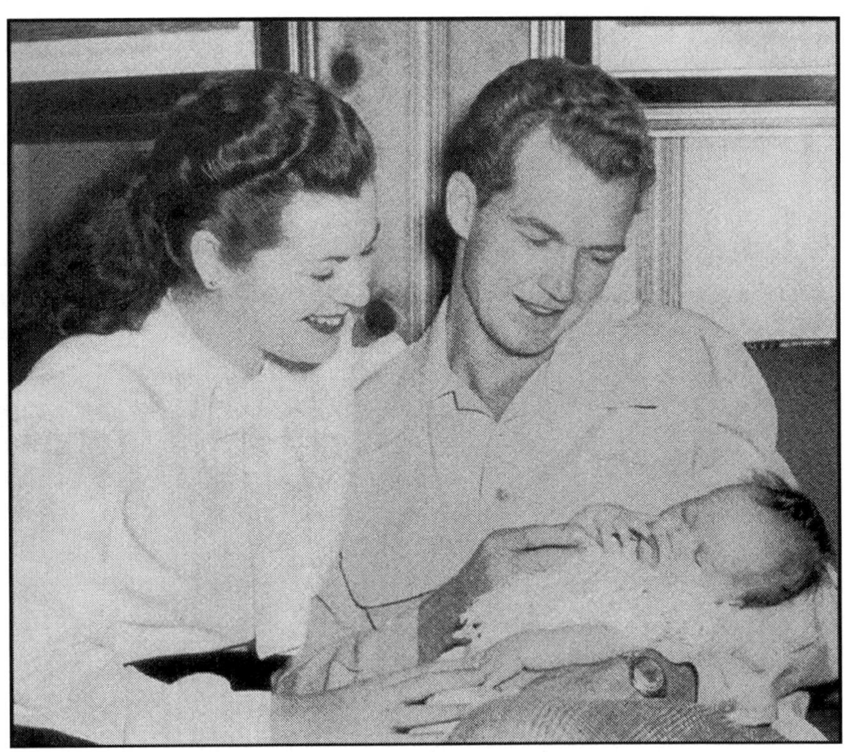

Jody was the biggest bright spot during a difficult time of career uncertainty caused by the confusion at RKO. For as far back as Barbara could remember, she loved kids. When she was still just a kid herself, Barbara couldn't believe her luck when she was old enough to help care for big sister Juanita's children, Jimmy and Diana. Go back to early press releases and you can find quotes like the one below.

"Her favorite things in the world, in the order of their importance are (1) babies; almost any baby will do, but she is especially ecstatic over her young nieces and nephews. She yearns for a flock of tots of her own."

Now that Barbara and Bill *did* have a child of their own, Barb was living the dream. But it came right on the heels of a nightmare. While Barb was pregnant, Bill was laid low by the same ailment that had made his stay in the service so brief. A painful back injury from his days as an acrobatic dancer resurfaced and he was unable to walk. On top of that, he came down with pleurisy! So there he was, stuck at home, and even if an acting job did come up, he couldn't take it.

It was Barbara who got him through all this. Bill was really down. As Barbara said, he wasn't the kind of guy who could hide his feelings. When he wasn't happy you could see it, and he definitely wasn't happy. Mostly, he was scared. Starting a new family wouldn't be easy if he couldn't work. Barbara was the one who kept him going through the months it took to recover. According to Bill, if one doctor couldn't figure out what to do, Barbara would find another. And if that doctor was stumped, Barb would find a specialist.

Meanwhile, *A Likely Story*, the movie that was supposed to spearhead a romantic comedy series for the young couple, came and went. Barbara and Bill handled their parts well, but the writing was weak and the story was overly complicated. Bill gets bumped on the head, thinks he's going to die, tries to commit suicide, finds himself rescued by

Barbara...and that's just in the first reel! On the plus side, the two of them made an adorable couple.

Sadly, there wouldn't be another Barb and Bill romantic comedy at RKO. New boss Dore Schary favored pictures with a message, which would provide future work for Barbara, but not for Bill. Meanwhile, Bill was growing more frustrated and he wasn't one to suffer in silence.

For one thing, he told Bob Thomas at AP that he didn't like the way he was being treated at RKO. He complained that, for the last several months, all he'd done was pose for pictures with Barbara. Thomas duly reported his complaint and perhaps that was one of the reasons he was offered a role in *The Window*, an excellent suspense/drama that cast

Barbara against type as a decidedly unglamorous struggling wife and mother with a child who has witnessed a murder. Unfortunately, Bill hadn't quite recovered from his health problems when first approached about being in the film, and had to bow out.

The Window required extensive shooting in New York City. Barbara didn't mind going to New York, but she wasn't going to leave the baby behind. So, little Jody and Bill were with Barbara when the movie began filming at RKO-Pathé's newly-constructed studio in Harlem and in abandoned tenements on 105th and 116th Streets. Barbara was fabulous in this boy-who-cried-wolf fable, which co-starred Arthur Kennedy and Bobby Driscoll.

Arthur Kennedy, Barbara & Bobby Driscoll

The movie supposedly takes place in the summer, but Barbara said it was freezing when they arrived in New York in November. When shooting outside scenes where the actors didn't have dialogue, Barbara said, "We'd have to hold our breath." And if they had to talk, "We'd put ice in our mouths, so the inside of our mouths would be as cold as it was outside," and hopefully keep the breath from showing.

Eventually, it was time to head back to Hollywood where the remainder of the interiors would be shot, but the new parents enjoyed their stay in New York, and what Barbara remembered most was that Jody began crawling while they were there!

That wasn't the only new development in the Hale family as 1948 arrived. If you believed the gossip columnists, it appeared mom and dad didn't want to work together anymore! In January, Jimmie Fiddler said Barb and Bill, now that they were married, objected to being teamed in pictures because "the public should not be given a chance to tire of them both, thereby cutting off their entire family income."

Huh? That doesn't make any sense. If they co-star in a movie together and it doesn't do well, they can simply make their next movies separately. Yet the same story was reported by other gossip gurus as well.

Erskine Johnson, in his "In Hollywood" column, said "Barbara and Bill have decided to go their separate ways, career wise. No more joint publicity and no more co-starring roles."

As similar stories appeared, it became clear someone was intent on spreading this report. Who was the most likely suspect? It would hardly be Barbara. She'd been quite busy making good films and receiving good notices. Bill, on the other hand, might have felt that he was too often in Barbara's shadow and needed a breakout film of his own.

If it was Bill, the leaks may have backfired. Some of the writers decided to expand on the blurb they had been given. For example, an article in the Portland Sunday Telegram added, "Barbara has somewhat outdistanced her husband in the Hollywood sweepstakes and is due for a build-up as a first rate dramatic star...her upward progress and popularity has been steady."

In any case, the disparity in film assignments for Barbara and Bill in 1948 remained the same. Barbara was given the female lead in Dore Schary's *The Boy With the Green Hair*, while Bill was assigned to a supporting role in the less impressive *A Woman's Secret*.

The Boy With Green Hair had a big name cast that included Pat O'Brien, Robert Ryan and Dean Stockwell. And Barbara was as lovely as ever playing kindly teacher Miss Brand.

Barbara became good friends with Robert Ryan on the picture, and she said they even talked about doing a play together. However, they never had free time at the same time. On the other hand, it was the prospect of too *much* free time that was on everybody's mind in the spring of 1948. In May, eccentric billionaire Howard Hughes took control of RKO He moved quickly. In July it was announced that Hughes would cut studio personnel by a whopping 75 percent!

By the fall, only three pictures were shooting on the lot, and one of then was *The Clay Pigeon*, co-starring Barbara and Bill.

The Clay Pigeon was actually the first film to be produced under the Hughes regime. The film noir was originally planned as a bigger project with Lawrence Tierney in Bill's role and Sid Rogell producing. Instead, Herman

Schlom, who worked with Barbara back in her *Gildersleeve* days and later with Barbara and Bill on *West of the Pecos*, handled producing chores. *The Clay Pigeon* was a good film, but this was a distressing time for RKO. It was even more distressing for RKO's contract players, since Hughes decided it was costing too much to keep them on the books!

"We were both fired like most everybody else when RKO went through a re-organization," said Barbara. "All our plans went flooey!" Bill was even more concerned than Barbara. "We were both out of work," he said, "and the savings account we had started so hopefully was beginning to look anemic. The studio ran through three administrations and everybody, including us, got fired." Bill, who had known poverty as a child, didn't ever want to see his daughter Jody forced to deal with it.

Barbara tried to ease her husband's fears. She pointed out that lots of other couples had children, even though they had far less security. And she also reminded Bill that losing their contracts at RKO wasn't exactly the worst thing in the world. Bill hadn't been happy there for quite some time, even complaining to a movie magazine that he had worked in front of a movie camera only 4 days in the previous 24 months! (That was for his small role in *A Woman's Secret*.)

The good news was, both Barbara and Bill had seen the Hughes shakeup coming, and they both tried to prepare for it. Barbara had lots of friends in the business, and she learned about a project at Columbia that she thought she'd be perfect for. The studio had a 1947 hit with a biography of famed singer Al Jolson. Sidney Buchman, Harry Cohn's right-hand man at Columbia, was now planning a follow-up and looking for a "wholesome-type" to play Jolson's wife.

"Wholesome," of course, was the word most frequently used to describe Barbara. So, she set about convincing Buchman she was the perfect person for the part. She succeeded. It turned out to be a win/win situation. The picture was a hit, Barbara got great reviews, and signed a long-term contract with Columbia.

Jolson Sings again certainly was a breakout picture. It was the highest grossing film of the year and received three Oscar nominations. Barbara went to New York for a week with the real Al Jolson to promote the movie. They did seven shows a day at various theaters and Barbara said Jolson loved performing for the live audiences, and gave his all. "They could hardly get Al off, because he loved to entertain," recalled Barbara. It was obvious that Jolson was in his element. Meanwhile, Barb said, she was exhausted after doing all the live shows and she couldn't keep up with him.

On Monday, May 22nd, 1950, Barbara and Jolson performed *Jolson Sings Again* on the *Lux Radio Theater.*

The first hint of what Barbara would do for her follow-up to *Jolson Sings Again* came in a short blurb from Hedda Hopper. "Evelyn Keys was suspended by Columbia for refusing *Baby Was Here* with Ronnie Reagan. So the part goes to Barbara Hale." Hopper had the basic story right, even though the title of the film and Barbara's co-star would change by the time it went into production. The title eventually became *And Baby Makes Three.* Columbia tried to borrow Ronald Reagan from Warner Bros., but he didn't want to do it. Instead, Robert Young, Barbara's co-star from *Lady Luck,* took the role. Bob considered Barbie a close friend by now. The two would relax behind the scene docks and chat between takes.

Perhaps Bob and Barb discussed script concerns. Reviews were mixed, but the New York Times said, "Robert Young and Barbara Hale, who are deserving of much better treatment, strive valiantly to keep this frail comedy alive."

Barbara's next film paired her with beloved actor Jimmy Stewart, and it turned out to be a lot of fun. *The Jackpot* was based on a true story. Stewart and wife Barb are thrilled when they answer a phone call and win $24,000 worth of merchandise from a radio quiz show. Their mood quickly changes, however, when they find they have to pay $7,000 in taxes on the items!

It's a very funny outing, and it reunited Barbara with James Gleason, the character actor who stood up for her when the director of *Lady Luck* tried to give her a hard time. A very young Natalie Wood also appears in the film. (Right)

Barbara, of course, had no way of knowing back then, that in just a few short years, Natalie Wood would be a movie star, appearing with Raymond Burr in the very adult movie, *A Cry in the Night.*

And there was certainly no way for Barb to predict that movie magazines would one day be trying to promote Natalie and Raymond as a hot item, but they did for a time.

Various pictures appeared showing Raymond squiring Natalie around town.

While, in the movie, Barbara was playing mom to Natalie and young Tommy Rettig, who would later gain fame on *Lassie*, she was also about to add to her own real-life family!

Barbara said, after little Jody was born, that she wanted to have more children. In fact, she said she was hoping for twins! Well, it didn't work out quite that way. But Barbara did learn she was pregnant again.

And, whether the new arrival was a boy or a girl, it would have an extra image of Barbara to stare at, even when mom was out of the room! Barbara got a bonus from *The Jackpot* in the form of a lovely painting. The gambling film showed

Barbara's portrait being painted. It would have been a shame to just store it in some dusty studio vault.

Luckily, the movie painting managed to find a perfect home!

Columbia's next Barbara Hale release was *Emergency Wedding*, a film that had actually been shot prior to *The Jackpot*. It was a remake of an earlier Barbara Stanwyck/Henry Fonda film called *You Belong to Me*. The New York Times wasn't too impressed with this newer version.

"This remake of a yarn about a millionaire, an insecure gent ludicrously jealous of his doctor-wife, is lightweight without being especially gay or serious. *Emergency Wedding*, except for a titter or two and an attempt to diagnose what ails organized medicine, is an unimpressive reproduction."

However, the film did reunite Barbara with Larry Parks. Barb was close to Larry's wife, Betty Garrett. And—as it turned out—Betty and Barbara had something in common. They soon learned they were pregnant at the same time! Below, the two expectant mothers hold a pow-wow.

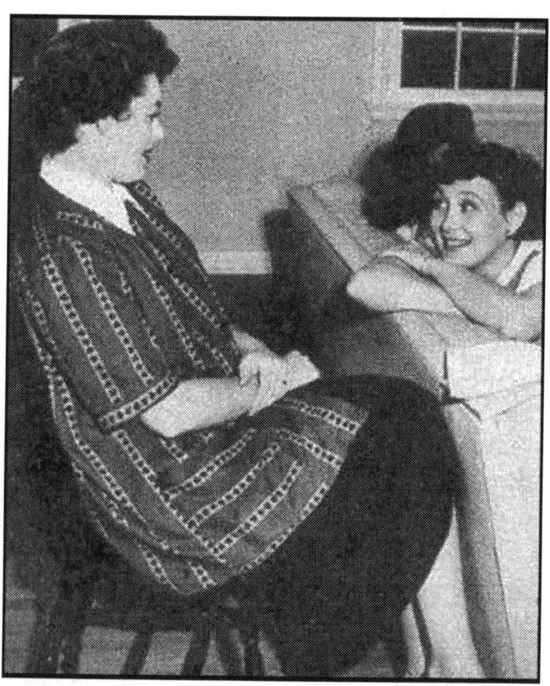

A GROWING FAMILY

The little cottage Barb and Bill bought while they were at RKO was fine when Jody was an only child. But they knew they were having more children, so they purchased a large lot in Van Nuys and began going over blueprints together.

It was a biggie! Below: Barb and Bill with the builder.

Bill's knowledge of construction engineering was a big plus. Inside what would become the living room, Barbara stands where she plans to have a sliding glass door installed. Behind Bill, a patio will be constructed and, eventually, a swimming pool will be added.

Barbara had originally hoped to put the pool in while they were building the house, but she realized it would bust the budget. So the frugal couple waited until after the new baby was born and put the pool in then. This was typical of Barbara and Bill.

It was a trait Raymond Burr, for one, admired. When Barbara was doing *Perry Mason* in 1962, Raymond said: "Barbara and Bill could be big spenders, I suppose, and live in a mansion in Bel-Air. But they prefer the more modest atmosphere of the San Fernando Valley and using their money to invest in real estate, which will benefit the family and give them security."

But *Perry Mason* was years away in 1950. Back then, Bill was busy building a house, and Barbara was overjoyed to learn she'd be having another baby. She had completed one additional film, *Lorna Doone*, in June. Her co-star was future TV *Robin Hood* Richard Greene.

Lorna Doone wouldn't be released for a full year and, by that time, Barbara had a new leading man in her life, little William Theodore Katt. He was born February 16, 1951. Little Billy, as his parents called him, would eventually decide to follow in the family tradition and become an actor. When Bill Katt was an adult and acting in TV and movies, Barbara suggested pumping up his acting credits. "I told Billy he should put on his resume that he was in *The Jackpot* and *Lorna Doone*." But Bill said 'Mother, I wasn't.' And

Barbara told him, "Oh yes, you were!" And Barbara was absolutely delighted to have another child.

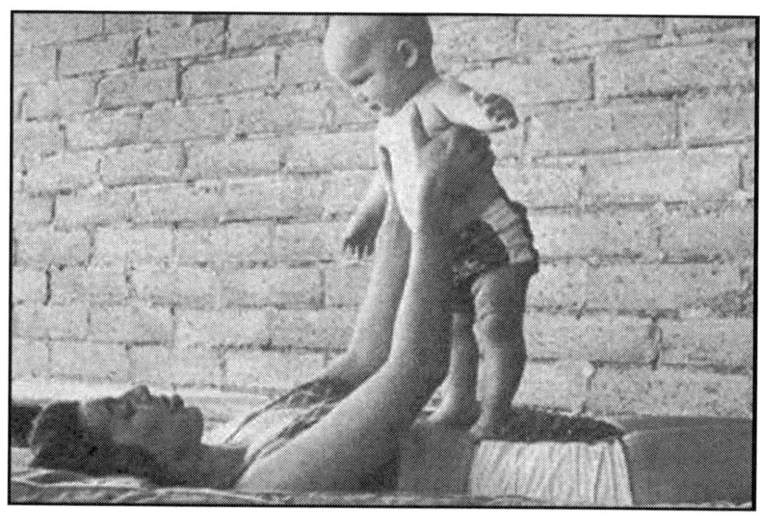

Meanwhile, dad dreamed of the day when he could pass his talent for carpentry and woodworking on to little Billy!

These were good times for Barbara. For a young woman whose greatest joy as a little girl was helping to raise her older sister's children and who wanted to go to art school so she could illustrate children's books or work for Walt Disney, having two children of her own was heaven.

Barbara had until the end of April before she had to report back to Colombia to shoot *The First Time* with Robert Cummings. Her former co-star Larry Parks was supposed to be the leading man, but he became a target of a controversial congressional investigation into alleged communist influence in motion pictures. It was the end of his Hollywood career, but he became a successful real estate investor.

Another dear friend of Barbara's, Jeff Donnell, *was* in the picture, though. They had met at RKO and would remain friends for the rest of their lives. Below, on one of the many publicity tours they did together.

Barb & Jeff with San Francisco policeman

In addition to Jeff Donnell, others in the solid supporting cast included veteran character actors like Paul Harvey and Cora Witherspoon. Best of all, *The First Time* was shot in less than four weeks, which meant Barbara was quickly back to spending full-time with the kids.

This was a big plus because "Daddy Bill," as Barb used to call him, was pretty busy himself around this time. Bill had been doing mostly low-budget pictures since leaving RKO, including several B-westerns. But B-westerns were being phased out because television was beginning to offer similar fare for free.

Bill saw the handwriting on the wall and, in a case of 'if you can't beat 'em, join 'em,' he signed on to do the early TV series *Kit Carson*, which quickly became a hit with kids.

Suddenly, Bill had something he'd wanted for years, stardom and recognition. Alright, it was mostly among the younger set, but the parents of his young fans noticed too.

There were newspaper and magazine articles and plenty of publicity from the show's sponsor, Coca Cola! Every TV supplement seemed to carry a picture of Bill in his new guise as a kid's television star!

Barbara was glad to see her husband getting more attention. She was an extremely intelligent woman, and she realized there had been times in the past when Bill felt he'd been treated as "Mr. Barbara Hale" by the press. The popularity of his new show went a long way toward easing those feelings. But Bill's schedule was grueling. They turned out one episode every two days, working six-day weeks! Luckily, Barbara had cut back on her schedule, leaving time for things like teaching Billy to say Grace.

It was a gift for Barbara to have this time with Billy and Jody. Soon, Barbara's own TV schedule would get in the way.

For now, though, Barbara was free until the end of the year. It gave her time to help Bill when the crazy *Kit Carson* schedule got the better of him. Barbara even had to drive over to the set one evening to provide emergency snacks. They were working until midnight and weren't allowed to break for supper!

The only plus side to the frantic pace of production, was that they shot a whole season's worth of shows in an incredible ten weeks! That gave Bill a long stretch in-between that he spent with Barbara, Jody, and little Billy.

Barbara didn't have to return to Columbia until the end of the year. She made a very brief cameo appearance in a film called *Rainbow 'Round My Shoulder*, and then had to head for Yuma, Arizona to do location work for her next film, *Last of the Comanches*. Barbara's co-stars in the film were Broderick Crawford and Lloyd Bridges. Brod, soon to begin his TV show *Highway Patrol*, had become rather portly. But Lloyd Bridges looked as slim and trim as ever. Below, from the film, Lloyd standing and Barbara on the ground.

Barbara said Bill got jealous of Bridges, packed Jody in the car and headed to the location to check things out for himself. (By this time, Barbara's mother was living near Barbara and Bill, so she could take care of little Billy.) Barbara had said Bill was quite sensitive, even back when they were dating, and anything that went wrong would bother him. Now he thought there was something very wrong indeed, and he was determined to go and check it out.

It must have been very embarrassing for Barb *and* for Lloyd Bridges. He and I met several years later and he struck me as a very nice guy, hardly deserving of being the target of jealous accusations.

The author with Lloyd Bridges

In one of those strange twists of fate that happen more often than we think, Lloyd's life intersected with Bill's in another way, just a few years after this incident. Williams turned down the lead in *Sea Hunt* because he didn't think TV viewers would be interested in an underwater show. Bridges accepted, and became a TV star when the show became a huge hit. Bill Williams would later star in a similar television show about a former Navy frogman, called *Assignment: Underwater*. But it was too little, too late and it lasted only one season.

After *The Last of the Comanches* cast and crew took a brief break for Christmas, they resumed shooting in Hollywood and the film wrapped March 3rd, 1952. Barbara now had most of March, April, May and June to relax with the family. By now, Jody was four and Billy was one.

At the end of June, Barbara had to go on location again, this time to Florida to shoot *Seminole*, with Rock Hudson, Anthony Quinn, Richard Carlson and Hugh O'Brian. Famed western director Bud Boetticher was at the helm and the film tried to give some insight into the Native American side of things, which was unusual for the time.

While Rock Hudson is the star, some of Barbara's most sensual scenes are with Anthony Quinn. If you only know Quinn from his post-*Zorba the Greek* films, it's quite a revelation to see him as a younger man with Barbara in his arms! And Barbara was about to be in an older man's arms too! Once she finished *Seminole*, Barb was bound for Colorado. *The Lone Hand* was shot in Durango, and rugged western star Joel McCrea was her leading man.

The uptick in location work for Barbara came at a time when Bill was getting more B-movie offers thanks to the popularity of *Kit Carson*. Barbara realized something had to be done about taking care of Jody and Billy. Up until then, she said, it seemed Bill was off when she was working and vice-versa. But with both of them busier, Barbara said:

"We discovered that we were asking too much of my mother, who had always been glad to baby sit. So we hired a housekeeper. At first, this worried me until I found I had a kind, sympathetic and perfectly reliable woman trustworthy of the care of our children. More important, she didn't try to push Bill or me out of our roles of Daddy and Mommy when we were home."

This must have been a difficult decision for Barbara. Here was a woman who, after babysitting for neighbors as a child, expressed a desire to become a nurse, so she could care for children. Now, she was turning the care of her *own* children over to somebody else. Here were two people who often said they would never have servants like other Hollywood couples, hiring a servant to watch over their little ones.

Barbara probably felt that she didn't have much choice if she and Bill were to continue their careers. And it must have seemed that she was doing something good for the kids. But, as you'll hear me say over and over again in this book, Barbara was an extremely intelligent woman, who had great insight. Barbara said she felt because she had only limited time with the children, she tried to use it in the most meaningful way possible. But she was aware of the pitfalls.

"The trouble is, with raising youngsters, you don't know if your theories have worked out for ten or twenty years, when they're grown. I can only pray that we're headed in the right direction, Bill and I. Time will tell."

Barbara's career was now flourishing on two fronts. In addition to films, she found herself in great demand in the burgeoning television industry. TV networks quickly realized that featuring well-known performers from motion pictures on their shows was a sure-fire way to attract viewers. And Barbara was, indeed, most attractive.

In November of 1952, Barbara appeared on the Ford Television Theater in the episode, *Change of Heart*. In it, she and co-star Stephen McNally try to cope with a teenager in trouble with the law. All three main characters, Barbara, McNally, and Darryl Hickman, were familiar actors from motion pictures.

And Barbara continued to do films. From late November until late December she was busy shooting *A Lion Is in the Streets* with James Cagney, a powerful film with an excellent cast that included Anne Francis, John McIntire and Frank McHugh.

A Lion Is in the Streets was released in September of 1953, just one month after an article appeared in a TV magazine indicating that Barbara's marriage had, at one point, been in trouble because Bill was jealous of her success. However, the magazine said, things were reportedly fine now, which was a blessing because Barbara was expecting another child. That part of the story was definitely true. Louella Parsons had revealed the stork rumor back in May.

Bur another part of the TV magazine story proved to be way off base. It hinted that Barb would soon be giving up acting. "Now that she is expecting a third heir, you can look for her to make home-life a career."

The truth was, while Barbara might dial back the number of films she did, she was just beginning a very active television career, which included the lead role in *Vacation for Ginny* on the *Schlitz Playhouse of Stars*.

BARBARA HALE STARS IN "VACATION FOR GINNY" ON "SCHLITZ PLAYHOUSE OF STARS" MAY 15

Carbara Hale plays a travel agency clerk who learns about life at a fancy resort in "Vacation for Ginny" on "Schlitz Playhouse of Stars" Friday, May 15, over the CBS-TV network (9:00-9:30 P.M., EDT).

By the end of the year, Barbara was preparing to receive the new addition to the family. Little Juanita Laura Lee

Williams was born on December 22, 1953. Mother and Baby were still in the hospital on Christmas day, so the family waited until they returned home for the big celebration!

Barbara took a nice long break to mark the baby's arrival. And Bill wasn't due to shoot the next season of *Kit Carson* for several months. He knew that, once he got into the frantic ten week period to grind out a whole season's worth of episodes, he'd have little time for anything else. "I leave the house about five in the morning," he said, "and I don't get back until eight or nine at night." So, before Bill got caught up in that crazy schedule, and before Barb accepted any more film work, they were able to enjoy some family time together.

Billy, Bill, Baby, Barbara, Jody

In the picture on the previous page, the newest addition to the family is referred to simply as "Baby." There's a reason for that. Bill favored the name "Juanita." Barb favored the name Laura Lee. The newspaper clipping below is proof that, early on, Barbara was winning.

Four-month-old Laura Lee Williams poses with mom, Barbara Hale, and dad, Bill Williams, TV's Kit Carson.

Actually, Barbara realized that even big sister Jody didn't like the name "Laura Lee," so "Juanita" eventually won out, but shortened to 'Nita. And, with another child in the household, there was the need for more room.

Once again, Bill's background in construction engineering came in helpful. He was able to come up with plans that would skillfully create an addition that would provide the necessary space, while blending in nicely with the existing architecture of the home. And, celebrities or not, Bill and Barbara had to submit an application for the new bedroom and bath they were adding, to the Los Angeles Building Department.

3

APPLICATION TO ALTER, REPAIR, or DEMOLISH AND FOR A Certificate of Occupancy

CITY OF LOS ANGELES DEPARTMENT OF BUILDING AND SAFETY — BUILDING DIVISION

Lot No. 20

Tract 9726

Location of Building 13909 Weddington St. Van Nuys

Between what cross streets? Ranchito + Hazeltine

Approved by City Engineer ... Deputy.

USE INK OR INDELIBLE PENCIL

1. Present use of building Dwelling Families 1 Rooms 6
2. State how long building has been used for present occupancy 3 years.
3. Use of building AFTER alteration or moving Dwelling Families 1 Rooms 8
4. Owner Mr + Mrs Bill Williams. Phone
5. Owner's Address 13909 Weddington St P. O. Van Nuys
6. Certificated Architect State License No. Phone
7. Licensed Engineer State License No. Phone
8. Contractor E. Joseph Minnecci State License No. 138976 Phone ST 92309
9. Contractor's Address 15718 Hartsook St. Encino
10. VALUATION OF PROPOSED WORK $5800.—
11. State how many buildings NOW on lot and give use of each. 1 Bldg. DWELLING
12. Size of existing building x Number of stories high 1 Height to highest point 14'
13. Material Exterior Walls wood + stucco. Exterior framework wood.
14. Describe briefly all proposed construction and work: add a 16'8" x 44'6" bedroom + bath – enclosing front porch. stucco + redwood exterior

NEW CONSTRUCTION

15. Size of Addition 16'8" x 44'6" Size of Lot ... Number of Stories when complete 1
16. Footing: Width 14" Depth in Ground 12" Width of Wall 6" Size of Floor Joists 2 x 6
17. Size of Studs 2x4 Material of Floor wood Size of Rafters 2 x 4 Type of Roofing SHAKE

I hereby certify that to the best of my knowledge and belief the above application is correct and that this building or construction work will comply with all laws, and that in the doing of the work authorized thereby I will not employ any person in violation of the Labor Code of the State of California relating to Workmen's Compensation Insurance.

Sign here Bill Williams (Owner or Authorized Agent)

By E. Joseph Minnecci

DISTRICT OFFICE

FOR DEPARTMENT USE ONLY

PLAN CHECKING | OCCUPANCY SURVEY | Investigation Fee $

TYPE OF RECEIPT | DATE ISSUED | TRACER No.

Barbara now had a house full of children, fulfilling her long-time dream. Bill had wide-spread recognition and loyal fans, giving him the self-confidence and reassurance he'd always sought. Things were perfect! And, of course, they were about to change.

BACK TO WORK

A film called *Unchained* marked Barbara's return to movies. It was shot in July of 1954 although it wasn't released until January of 1955. The film itself was a decent prison reform drama, but it is best remembered today for its popular theme song, *Unchained Melody*. Originally, Al Hibbler, Les Baxter and Roy Hamilton charted with the song. But it became a hit all over again when performed by the Righteous Brothers, most notably after it was featured in the film, *Ghosts*. It's nice to report that there is a familiar face on early sheet music for this all-time classic.

After *Unchained*, Barbara spent the rest of the summer of 1954 shooting *The Far Horizons*, a rather fanciful retelling of the story of the Lewis and Clark expedition.

Fred MacMurray and Charlton Heston co-starred.

And, before the year was out, Barbara filmed an episode of the *Ford Television Theater* with Dane Clark and Cleo Moore.

Two motion pictures and a TV show in the course of a year may not sound all that extraordinary, until you remember that this is a woman who had just given birth to a newborn as the year got underway! And her schedule for the following year would make 1954 seem like a walk in the park!

Barbara was all over the small screen in 1955 and also made one of her most interesting movies. On TV, she appeared once again on the *Schlitz Playhouse*, in an episode that also featured Frances Bavier, later to gain fame as "Aunt Bee" on *The Andy Griffith Show*. She also shot an interesting episode of *Science Fiction Theater* that co-starred Hugh Beaumont, soon to play Ward Cleaver, the father on the successful sitcom *Leave it to Beaver*.

Next, Barbara was reunited with Jimmy Stewart in *The Windmill*, an episode of *General Electric Theater*, hosted by Ronald Reagan. Somehow, Barbara also squeezed-in *The Hastings Secret*, another episode of *Science Fiction Theater* that co-starred her husband Bill and future *Perry Mason* judge Morris Ankrum.

There's an important topic that needs to be discussed here, because it affected the dynamic of Barbara and Bill's marriage. Science Fiction Theater provides one of the most clear-cut examples of the disparity in Barb and Bill's careers, even in these pre-*Perry Mason* days.

When Barbara did her first *Science Fiction Theater*, the one with Hugh Beaumont, she was paid $1,750. For her next, the one with husband Bill, their salaries were lumped together and the total came to $2,750. You would assume that this meant Barbara was getting $1,175 and Bill was getting $1,000. But, in later episodes when Bill worked solo, he usually got only $800. This had been going on back in the studio days as well and, over the years, Bill offered contradictory statements about it. Early on, he said he held the traditional view that the man should support the family.

But later, Bill said, "As for that old bugaboo about who makes more money than whom, we don't care. It all goes into the same bank account." Was that true? I doubt it. I think Bill meant it when he said it. But, the truth is, he never would have brought the subject up if it didn't bother him.

At any rate, he had to work harder and harder to keep up with Barbara. After finishing her *Science Fiction Theater* with Bill, she worked with him again on an extremely spooky episode of *Studio 57* called *Young Couples Only*, and went on to appear solo on *Screen Director's Playhouse, Celebrity Playhouse*, and *Climax*. And that's just her TV output! It doesn't include her movie, *The Houston Story*.

The film may not answer the question, "Do Blondes Have More Fun," but it makes it clear that, when the blonde in question is Barbara, she looks *very* sexy! Barbara shot the movie in 1955, but it wasn't released until February of 1956.

And 1956 would be a crucial year for Barbara, although there was nothing unusual about the way it began. Barb shot the film *The 7th Cavalry* with Randolph Scott from January 12th until February 3rd.

The rest of the winter and most of the spring was devoted to television projects. A *Damon Runyon Theater* with former movie *Perry Mason* Donald Woods and *Houston Story* co-star Gene Barry, an episode of *Television*

Theater with Dane Clark called *Behind the Mask*, and *The Guardian*, an episode of the TV anthology series *Star Stage*. Barbara also appeared on the inspirational program *Crossroads*, in an episode that featured Regis Toomey (later to appear in two episodes of *Perry Mason*,) and Max Showalter (later to appear on *Perry Mason* six times.)

Next, Barbara did an episode of the popular show *The Millionaire*, playing twins. Husband Bill co-starred.

Barbara had two other projects in 1956. One was a *Playhouse 90*. The other was just a pilot for a TV series. It was shot rather inexpensively at the Fox Western Avenue lot using sets left over from previous movies. The pilot's main office set, "borrowed" from the movie *The Man in the Grey Flannel Suit*, was already becoming outdated. The "star" was best known for playing bad guys and, worst of all, with westerns all the rage, the show was about a lawyer! What chance could this pilot possibly have?

DESTINED TO BE DELLA

Barbara was talented in a number of areas and, on occasion, she looked into ways she could make some money from home and spend less time at the studio. After Jody was born, she was in talks with a company to sell baby dresses that she designed. And she also planned to design dolls and sell them through an actress -friend's high-end Beverly Hills children's boutique.

The Boutique was called "The Enchanted Cottage," and the actress-friend was Gail Patrick Jackson. Her husband was the literary agent for Erle Stanley Gardner, creator of *Perry Mason.* Gardner liked and trusted Gail and put her in charge of a projected show about the character. Gail felt sure she knew the best person to play Della Street.

There was, however, one little problem. Barbara didn't want to do a series. She was away from the kids enough and she felt a series would really tie her down. But Gail pulled out all the stops in trying to convince Barb to take the part. She gave her a script, Barbara read it and liked it, but noted that whoever they chose to play Mason would probably die from exhaustion. He had three-quarters of the lines in the script!

It was then that Gail told Barbara, Raymond Burr would play the lead.

Barbara knew if anybody could pull it off, Raymond could. "Raymond was one of the first people I met at RKO," Barbara said. "I had known him since the first day I arrived in

Hollywood." Barbara also recalled years later, that the first time she laid eyes on Raymond she thought, "Oooh ... he's the most handsome man I've ever seen!"

So Barbara was more than happy with her leading man and loved the script. That meant her only remaining concern was about being away from the kids even more than she was already. Gail countered this objection by telling Barbara the show wasn't likely to run more than 18 episodes anyway!

What? How could anybody in 1956 not realize *Perry Mason* was going to be a sure-fire hit? I had the same question until Perry Mason *himself* explained it to me.

The author with Raymond Burr

I spoke with Raymond almost 20 years after the original show had ended, almost 30 years after it first went on the air. The first thing he emphasized was what a chance "Paisano Productions," (Erle Stanley Gardner, Gail Patrick and Gail's husband) took by insisting on an hour-long show. Raymond reminded me that most mystery/drama shows in those days ran only a half-hour, and nobody knew if viewers would sit still for a whole 60 minutes. Always humble, Raymond was also concerned that he didn't have the necessary "star" power to carry a show.

We know now that those worries were unfounded, but back then, I think Gail Patrick was being honest when she told Barbara the show was likely to have a limited run. Another plus for Barbara was that her character, Della Street, wouldn't be too confusing for the kids. "I liked that she wasn't married," Barbara said. "My husband didn't have to see me every week married to another man, and our children didn't have to see me mothering other children." So, Barbara agreed to do the pilot we mentioned earlier, which was shot October 3rd through the 9th, 1956.

In another sign that few people back then had any idea that *Perry Mason* would ever be the classic that we know and love today, it took a long time for the network to decide whether it would go ahead with the series, and an even longer time to get sponsors for it. It was six months between the time they shot the pilot in 1956 and the time they began shooting regular shows in mid-April of 1957.

As usual, Barbara had no intention of remaining idle while she waited for *Perry Mason* to gear up for regular production. In March, she and Bill signed with Universal to appear in *Slim Carter*, a film about an orphan boy who helps transform a cowboy singer/actor with feet of clay into a real hero. Barbara and Bill's roles amount to extended cameos, as they portray a former actress and her movie photographer husband, celebrating their silver wedding anniversary on the set of a film. Of special interest is the appearance of Bill Hopper in this movie with Barb, just a month before they'd start shooting regular episodes of *Perry Mason* together.

Bill Williams, Bill Hopper, Barb by cake.

Once they did begin regular production of *Perry Mason* things moved quickly. By the time the show actually made its debut on Sept 21, 1957, more than a dozen episodes had already been filmed. More importantly, Barbara, Raymond, William Hopper, Bill Talman and Ray Collins looked like they'd been working together all of their lives.

Perhaps the biggest surprise was the remarkable chemistry between Barbara and Raymond. Somehow, when they looked at each other, the romantic sum of their charisma equaled even more than its parts. It had been that way from their very first appearance together on the pilot, below, when Raymond's hair was shorter and the producers hadn't yet learned that Barbara needed very little makeup.

This aura of attraction only grew in ensuing episodes, creating an "Are they or aren't they" guessing game among viewers. It certainly wasn't something you could buy and bottle. If it was, every producer in Hollywood would have been out there searching for it. Ironically, though, it was something Erle Stanley Gardner didn't really want. He hoped to play down any romance and Barbara knew why.

"He was going with his secretary," said Barbara, "but he was married to a Catholic woman." She didn't want a divorce and he didn't want to give up the girl friend. Barbara said Gardner felt, as Della, she was basically playing his girlfriend/secretary, and he didn't want any hints of hanky-panky. As Barbara jokingly said, "I was the bad girl!"

As they got further into that first season, it became obvious that *Perry Mason* was going to require a great deal of time and effort on the part of everyone involved. The burden was heaviest on Raymond, because he had so much dialogue in every show. He had to sleep at the studio during the week, because the shooting schedule didn't leave time to drive home every night.

Barbara got home every night, but she also found herself working more than she had anticipated. She left the house early in the morning and often didn't return until late at night. And she had to find time to squeeze in publicity appointments, too. It was a far cry from what she envisioned before beginning the show. Back then, she had tried to convince herself that accepting the *Perry Mason* commitment would be positive for Jody, Billy and 'Nita.

"Actually, I looked on the series as being good for the children. Why? Because they need the security of knowing they will see their mother at certain definite hours. On a series, I can give them that knowledge, whereas when I'm doing only occasional shows, they never know when to expect me home. For children our youngsters' age, this uncertainty is no good." (Jody was ten at the time, Billy was six, and 'Nita was four.)

But these words were spoken by Barbara before *Perry Mason* aired. She was interviewed for an issue of *TV Radio Mirror* that came out the summer prior to the show's premiere. And, looking back, it seems clear Barbara's assessment of the situation was overly optimistic. She was often leaving early in the morning, before the kids were off to school, and getting back after the kids returned. The worse it got, the more film magazines claimed the family managed to cram a year's worth of quality time into every weekend. One article said Barbara rushed home from church on Sundays, hastily made sandwiches, and drove to a quiet part of the San Fernando Valley so the family could ride bikes together!

The article doesn't explain how, after the ride, Barbara packed the family, the bikes and the picnic leftovers up, drove home, washed the kids, had dinner, put the children to bed and then studied her lines for the next day!

It was the same with fan magazine articles about the kids at home. You'd think their yard was some kind of summer camp. Don't get me wrong, the place was beautiful and it was perfect for growing children. But from the pictures in the magazines, you'd think Barbara and Bill spent every waking moment playing with the kids.

In truth, Barbara and Bill were too busy working to spend a great deal of time with the kids. I stumbled on something when I was re-reading the *TV Radio Mirror* article from this period. Somehow, I'd missed it before, and I'm almost sorry I found it, because there's a tinge of sadness...a feeling of "what if." At one point, talking about the lack of time she and Bill had with the children, Barbara said, "Our dream is retirement in five years, so we can really enjoy and devote time to the kids when we feel they will most need our direction. Jody will then be fifteen, Billy eleven, 'Nita nine." Barbara said that in 1957, just as Perry Mason was beginning its TV run. The next time she talked about spending more time with the kids was in 1966 after the show finished its run. By then, Jody was nineteen. And, as Billy who was then fifteen pointed out, 1966 was a little late in the day to talk about retiring to spend more time with the "kids."

Bill Jr. inherited both his good looks and an extremely intelligent mind from his parents. In musing on "what if things had been different," he came up with a scenario that made a great deal of sense. Knowing his father had a good head for business, he speculated that if his dad had gone into the production end of movies, it might have eliminated much of the friction in the marriage. And, as young Bill said in the book *Hollywood's Star Children* by Raymond Strait, "I don't think my mother should ever have done the *Perry Mason* television series. I would have had her remain in films, because she was getting better and better and had made some terrific films. She was a fine actress, and that series just ate her up."

It's a tough position to be in for those of us who love *Perry Mason*: knowing that Bill Jr. may well be right as far as his family is concerned, but realizing what the rest of us would have missed if Barbara had turned down the role.

Perhaps your family was like mine. *Perry Mason* helped bring us together. My brother and I were young, but we really enjoyed this program that our parents loved to watch every week. And thinking about it all these years later still brings back fond memories. I'm sure that's true for many of us.

There's no denying now, however, that those memories came at a price for Barbara and her family. The *Perry Mason* schedule was a killer, both for Raymond and for Barbara, and it soon became obvious that Gail Patrick Jackson's prediction of a short run for the series was in error. The show just kept getting more popular as the chemistry between Barbara and Raymond became more evident.

And, despite Erle Stanley Gardner's edict that there be no, as he put it, "hanky-panky" between Della and Perry, that didn't stop viewers from speculating about what *might* be going on. It was hard *not* to because there seemed to be something so special in the way they interacted, almost as if they had their own little secret and they weren't going to let us in on it. If someone asked me to do an encyclopedia entry on the relationship between Raymond and Barbara, I wouldn't actually *write* anything. I'd simply display any picture that captured them in unguarded moments.

I can't help thinking of an outtake from what began as a serious publicity photoshoot. Barbara had been given a notebook and was supposed to look every bit the efficient secretary. Raymond was to represent the perfect, dignified attorney. What happened? The outtake shows Raymond deciding, at the last minute, to take a bite out of Barbara's notebook, and Barbara collapsing in laughter on his chest.

The publicity people finally did get the picture they wanted, but not before a little more clowning around by

Barbara and Raymond. Scenes like these, so often playful, provocative and flirtatious, were just another example of how comfortable Barbara and Raymond were with each other.

There were several reasons for the easy warmth and understanding the two of them shared, most of which are covered in my books *Remembering Perry Mason with Raymond Burr*, and *Perry Mason, A Love Story*. But one factor that doesn't seem to get much attention is the relationship between Barbara and Bill during the run of the program. Things were very different from when they first met. When the two young hopefuls first got together at RKO, passing on the lot or having coffee in the commissary, it was almost as if they needed to find each other.

Many actors, who are able to communicate with thousands of people on the screen, have trouble one-on-one.

Bill and Barbara had been a bit like that, each of them needing, as Bill put it, "a shoulder to lean on," as they tried to cope with their new found fame. Bill was able to honestly share the story of his difficult childhood with Barbara, who was compassionate and caring. And Barbara, despite all her outward assurance, also needed someone she could confide in. Although she had expressed the extent of her homesickness to some of her girlfriends, Bill—who never really had a home—seemed to understand best.

But that was then. By the time *Perry Mason* came along, troubles had long been brewing. Luckily, she had Raymond and a close circle of friends in her life who were there for her.

But things at home continued to deteriorate even as *Perry Mason* was enjoying its greatest success in the ratings. As always, Barbara was resourceful in facing the situation.

Around this time, several stories popped up in the press indicating the *Perry Mason* star was having problems at home. The one that got the most attention, because it had a catchy title and concluded with a positive spin, appeared in *TV Radio Mirror* in September of 1962.

RAYMOND BURR SAVED MY MARRIAGE

It was obvious to the "Perry Mason" cast: Barbara Hale was seriously troubled. But why? There was only one man in her life, Bill Williams, her husband now for (Continued on next page)

and love again..."

Despite the sensational title, the gist of the story was simple: Bill was jealous of Barbara's success and was making life miserable at home. I believe that one of the sources was Jeanne Cooper, the actress who played Katherine Chancellor on the soap opera *The Young and the Restless*. She and Barbara were extremely close and parts of the article sound a lot like things Jeanne was saying about the relationship between Barb and Bill. Jeanne was undoubtedly getting it from Barbara and the fact that the story was leaked was no accident.

Moreover, what most people don't know is that the same basic story had been leaked earlier, with what appeared to be a message to Bill to change his ways or a divorce might be in the offing! In a July 30th interview with Hank Grant for his *TV Time* column, Barbara stayed mostly on topic answering questions about how she raised a family while devoting so much time to *Perry Mason*. "To some, getting up at 5:30 every morning is a dreadful bore, like punching a timeclock," she said. "To me, (compared to the uncertainty of movie schedules,) it's a blessing. The children know exactly when their mother will come home and they've also settled into a comfortable routine with a housekeeper to care for them when I'm at work."

The interviewer pressed, asking Barbara whether she felt the children fully accepted the situation, and here's where she seemed to lump husband Bill in with the children.

"I don't believe any child completely accepts a working mother," she said. "But a child also never completely accepts that he can't have three ice cream cones before dinner. *But there have also been a few times when my husband grouched about my working, but those times were fleeting bursts of displeasure that could have been occasioned by something entirely irrelevant.* [italics added]

The interviewer then goes out of his way to give Barbara a chance to pull back on her criticism of Bill, by throwing her a softball question designed to elicit a positive response. He mentions the "ideal" state of their marriage and remarks on how unusual that is among couples in the acting profession. Instead of gushing about how wonderful the marriage is,

Barbara gives an answer that sounds very much like a warning shot being fired across the bow!

"Bill and I have been married for 15 years," she said, "but I never take anything for granted. This is chapter 15. Who knows what chapter 16 will bring?"

Think about what Barbara is saying here and how unhappy she must have been to say it in a public forum. The translation is rather simple. "Look, it's true we've been married for quite a few years, but don't take it for granted that we'll be married next year!"

Meanwhile, newspaper clippings containing candid photos hardly reflect a carefree couple.

The jealousy problem had been there for years. At times Bill felt like he was "Mr. Barbara Hale." He talked about the time he went back east with Barbara for the opening of her movie, *The Window*. The studio publicity people met them at the train and whisked Barbara away. Later, when he arrived at the hotel and mentioned a reservation in the name of Mr. and Mrs. Bill Williams, they didn't know what he was talking about. Then it occurred to Bill to say it might be in the name of Barbara Hale. "We do have a Barbara Hale registered," the clerk said suspiciously. "Do you know her?" At this point, Bill had about had it. "I ought to," he snapped. "She's the mother of my child!"

Bill and Barbara went through some rough times, no doubt about it, and providing Bill with roles on *Perry Mason* wasn't a permanent fix. He was a talented man, but like so many actors who got into the business around the same time, after the war ended, roles were hard to come by. He worked hard, took whatever he could find, always did a professional job and gained fame on *Kit Carson*. He was a frequent guest star on episodic television and delivered impressive performances. But, despite all that, he always seemed to be in Barbara's shadow.

Bill Williams retired from acting in the early eighties, and then devoted his time to one of his other main interests, the building business, in which he was quite talented. He was 77 years old when he was transported from his desert home to St. Joseph's Medical Center in Burbank, where he died of complications from a brain tumor on September 21, 1992.

MAKING NEW MEMORIES

The Case of the Careless Kidnapper is one of the all-time favorite episodes of the original *Perry Mason* among fans, because it's so direct about the relationship between Perry and Della. On a lovely moonlit night, they're in a garden outside a home where a party is taking place. They've been invited to it, but they're stalling, obviously not wanting to give up this private moment together.

Perry says, "Della, when was the last time you went to a nightclub, drank champagne and danced 'til dawn?" Della gets a wistful look in her eyes and tells him it's been so long that she can barely bring back the memory. "All right then," says Perry, "Let's create some new memories!"

"You're the boss," says Della with a big smile on her face.

Then the two of them turn, Perry puts his arm around Della, and they walk into the night.

I saw the episode when it first aired on April 30, 1964. Little did I know then, that some 20 years later I'd be sitting with an enthusiastic Raymond and hearing about the "new memories" he and Barbara were finally getting a chance to make!

Raymond had long wanted to do a two hour version of *Perry Mason.* He felt that anytime one of the original hour-long shows was based on an Erle Stanley Gardner novel (which was most of the time,) viewers were short-changed. "We were never able to get all of Erle Stanley Gardner's clues and all the other good things he put into his books into one show," he told me.

Raymond also said his other big condition was that Barbara co-star. He had just finished making the first of the

Perry Mason TV movies in Canada, and I remember how very happy he was. He was so thrilled, not just to be working with Barbara again, but to be working with her *in the role of Della.* He was quick to point out that they had worked together on other shows in between, including *Ironside.*

Barbara and Raymond on *Ironside*

But Raymond told me working with Barbara on the first *Perry Mason* TV movie was different. He said the years just seemed to melt away when he looked across at Barbara in the courtroom on that first day of filming. And there was something else he said to me that day that struck me as odd at the time, but now makes more sense. He said working with Barbara on *Perry Mason* again was like "wiping away twenty years of *not altogether good times.*" It was similar to an even stronger statement that later showed up in a magazine article. Raymond said coming back to *Perry Mason* with Barbara after all those years meant that "*suddenly all the terrible things that have happened are gone* and you are doing all the lovely things you were doing long ago." It was obvious that the lovely things he was talking about doing years ago, involved working with Barbara on the original show.

Shooting a scene on the old Fox backlot

I kept wondering what was so bad about the years after the original *Perry Mason* and before the new *Perry Mason*

TV movies. The answer finally came after I spoke with one of Barbara's close friends. She told me that Barbara used to talk frequently about how much she loved working with Raymond on *Perry Mason*...how close everyone was, how much they enjoyed each other, both cast and crew, and how much she missed it. That's almost exactly what Raymond had told me. "We all ended up being very close friends," he said. "We were very fortunate there...the crew as well as the actors."

So I believe what was "so bad" about the years between the two *Perry Masons*, was simply that Barbara and Raymond weren't working together on *Perry Mason*! I know it sounds crazy, since Raymond's schedule was beyond belief and Barbara's wasn't far behind back then. But I think they both came to view those years as some of the best of their lives.

Now, Barbara and Raymond were getting a second chance...a kind of do-over...only this time, without so much pressure. They say you can never go home again, but you can certainly give it a hell of a try, and that's exactly what Barbara and Raymond did, much to the delight of fans everywhere.

And any concerns about whether viewers would accept Perry and Della all these years later were quickly laid to rest, when the initial TV movie was the number one show across the country and the highest rated TV movie of the year!

Barbara was also thrilled to have her son Bill playing "Paul Drake, Jr.," on the initial episodes of the show.

Barbara with son as Paul Drake Jr.

A woman who was very close friends with both Barbara and young Bill, told me it was almost as if they were in some kind of competition doing the show, each trying to encourage the other to do their best. And I remember Raymond telling me how proud he was of this young fellow he'd known as a child, doing such a fine job as a grown actor. Bill left after getting an offer to do a show of his own, which unfortunately, wasn't successful. In all, he had played Paul Drake Jr. in nine *Perry Mason TV Movies.*

The original Paul Drake, William Hopper, had passed away in 1970. Barbara dearly missed him, and other members of the original cast. Ray Collins, who played Lt. Tragg, was special to her. When his memory was faltering, she used to help him run his lines before scenes. Barbara was fond of Bill Talman too, but she later claimed he almost got her into a lot of trouble. According to Barbara, Talman offered her a ride home, explaining he just had a brief stop to make on the way. Luckily, Barb's husband was picking her up. It was the night Bill got busted at a nude pot party!

Friends told me that, for all the fun she had doing the later television movies, there was one downside. If she knew you well, Barbara would admit, privately, that it was getting harder. When she started the original show, Barbara was in her mid-thirties. When she began the TV movies Barbara was in her sixties. She looked much younger than her age, but the years still slow us all down a bit.

Raymond, meanwhile, was several years older than Barbara, and had a weight problem that was taking a toll. But, like Barbara, he wasn't going to let anything get in the way of returning to *Perry Mason.*

Sure, they were older, but they were also wiser. And they had more freedom. Erle Stanley Gardner had passed away and they no longer felt bound by his edicts against romance. And yes, Raymond and Barbara did manage to get a very satisfying kiss into one of the shows, *The Case of the Telltale Talk Show Host.*

Barbara said, after all these years, Raymond was family. And Raymond felt the same way. "I'm fortunate," he said. I don't have lots of close friends, but the ones I do have, (like Barbara,) are patient and understanding."

Raymond Burr finished his last TV movie with Barbara in Mid-August of 1993. He passed away less than a month later. His death left a big hole in Barbara's life.

THE DEFENSE RESTS

Remember how most episodes of Perry Mason ended? Having done his usual fantastic job, Perry has forced the culprit to admit guilt, good triumphs over evil, and Barbara, Perry, and Paul go back to the office, where somebody tells a joke, everybody laughs and we fade to the closing credits.

Wouldn't it be great if things were like that in real life? Of course, they're not. Life is rarely that simple. Barbara said she used to laugh when she'd see a picture of herself on the cover of some magazine looking like the epitome of glamour, and knowing that was hardly the way she really dressed at home. After completing the last of the *Perry Mason TV Movies*, Barbara decided it was time for the defense to rest.

Her cohorts on defense team...Raymond, Bill Hopper, William Talman and Ray Collins...were already gone.

Raymond had been the last one to go and the toughest on Barbara. During the final show with Raymond, it was so hard to keep from crying...not wanting him to see her so worried about him. But she managed to get through that last one with Raymond and a few others later with "guest lawyers," that she promised Raymond she'd do just to keep the crew working.

During Barbara's final years, she was comforted by so many wonderful memories, including 1959's Emmy win as Best Supporting Actress.

Barbara with her Emmy

But don't let her show business triumphs fool you. Barbara had had her share of hard knocks over the years too. You don't hear about them, because she rarely talked about them.

Being promised a part, only to be told at the last minute you weren't getting it, was one of the hazards of the business, and Barbara had first-hand experience.

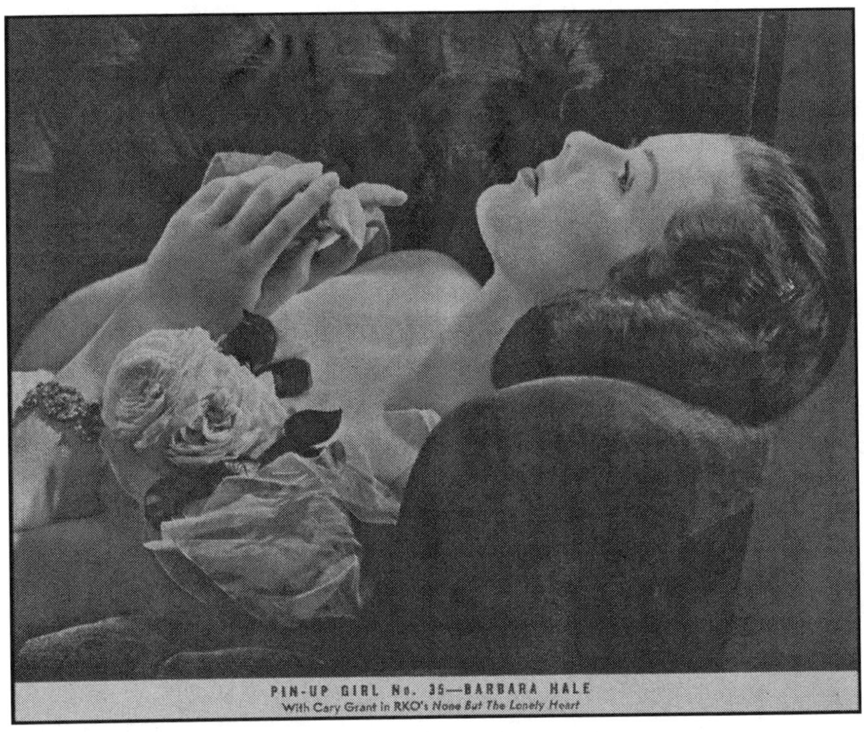

PIN-UP GIRL No. 35—BARBARA HALE
With Cary Grant in RKO's *None But The Lonely Heart*

The caption says Barbara is starring with Cary Grant in *None But the Lonely Heart*. The announcement was premature. Barbara was supposed to appear in the film and RKO wanted her to do the picture. But British backers involved with the film had other ideas. Perhaps it's just as well. The rather grim, downbeat movie was one of the few Cary Grant films to actually lose money!

Barbara had several fights like this over the years, many of which she won. Make no mistake about it, she didn't make it in this rough and tumble business by being a pushover. I've heard others who loved her, echo the sentiments of a co-worker at Columbia: "Barbara's was the easiest sort of temperament to work with. She was always agreeable. But don't ever push her. Under her soft exterior is a will of steel."

True, Barbara could be tough, but that never interfered with the amazing number of long-term friendships she maintained. Barbara's inner circle included Betty White, Beverly Garland of *My Three Sons* fame, and Jeanne Cooper of *The Young and the Restless*. Fans would be surprised at the "earthy" discussions these gals had at the old *Tail 'o the Cock restaurant* or in gatherings at their homes! And, even in her later years, those who knew Barbara well, say she enjoyed the fact that men were attracted to her, and loved to do a little harmless flirting! All of these silver screen icons *thought* young, so they *stayed* young. They were like a second family. With them, Barbara could discuss the very real problems that she, like everyone else, faced.

Being a star doesn't protect you from life's little ups and downs, nor does it render you immune to the big ones. The troubles in Barbara's marriage didn't magically go away. In later years, Bill spent much of his time in their Palm Desert house, while Barbara mostly lived in Sherman Oaks. Barb's place was decorated in a comfy, old fashioned style. The décor at Bill's was more typical of the swinging seventies, complete with wet bar, light leather sofa, and shag carpet. About the only reminder of Barbara at the house were the Amana appliances, because it was built when Barb was a commercial spokeswoman for the firm.

And it wasn't just her own marriage Barbara worried about. The problems in her parents' marriage, although they were never revealed to outsiders, were another source of sadness. The loving, rural family that provided the fairy-tale wedding in the fairy-tale church didn't have a fairy-tale marriage in real life. Barbara's mother and father were good people, but they eventually went their separate ways. Barbara's mom moved down to North Hollywood to be near Barbara, while her dad stayed back in Rockford.

It was there, in 1957, that Mr. Hale—by then in another relationship—became the father of twins, giving Barbara two half-brothers! Like so many holdovers from the old Hollywood publicity days, anything that might be inconvenient quickly disappeared. To this day I don't think most people have any idea that Barbara had these additional, much younger, siblings.

Having seen the many public relations pictures of Barbara's children in this book, you can probably understand why I didn't ask to interview them. It seems to me they had to do enough publicity work as kids to last a lifetime. Bill is the one you're probably most familiar with, since his acting talents have been on display for many years. Perhaps you first saw him in the films *Carrie* or *Big Wednesday*, or on his hit TV series *The Greatest American Hero*. Then again, maybe you caught him in the *Perry Mason* TV movies where he played Paul Drake, Jr., helping his mom and Raymond solve a fresh batch of mysteries.

But it couldn't have been easy growing up in a home where publicity considerations were such an all-important factor. It seemed "little Billy" showed up in almost every picture taken at their home, and it must have been hard for the youngster to have to "share" his father with so many other kids.

In 1955, the TV supplement of a local newspaper said the following of big Bill: "Wherever he goes kids gather in swarms around Bill. Even at home, if he wheels the lawn mower out of the garage, word spreads quickly that "Kit Carson" is outside and soon he has a sizeable audience of fans. Bill always has time to talk to the youngsters, and with three children of his own, he's deeply conscious of the importance of making the right kind of impression on young minds."

One day Billy actually got into an autograph line outside the house, and when he got to his father, without looking up his dad said, "Who do you want the autograph made out to?" Little Billy replied, "It's me, your son, dad." Growing up in a show business family wasn't easy!

Bill once said that perhaps it would have been better if his mom and dad had divorced, but he quickly walked that back. I think he realized his parents were human, they had their differences, but they did the best they could.

Bill's older sister Jody, as the first born, had to endure posing for publicity pictures the longest. It began when she was an infant in 1947 and didn't end until the *Perry Mason* years, when the poor kid was an adolescent! But she got through it and grew up to be the kind of person I'm sure Barbara would be proud of.

Barbara's youngest, 'Nita, worked as a lighting stand-in for Barb on the *Perry Mason* TV Movies. Barbara helped raise Nita's two children and was extremely close to Bill's as well. "Becoming a grandmother has been one of the most gratifying experiences of my life," she said.

But even for someone like Barbara, who was the first to admit she led a charmed life, there were setbacks along the way. Not long after Raymond died, she discovered she had cancer. There was a blockage in her intestines that had to be removed, but the operation appeared to be successful. Barbara had to undergo chemotherapy however, in an attempt to make sure the cancer didn't spread to the colon. At the time, young Bill said his mom's courage and determination were an inspiration.

In 1997, unfortunately, it became clear that the cancer had come back. Once again, Barbara did what needed to be done. She entered the hospital and underwent surgery. And, once again, her courage was on display. She lived for another 20 years.

Barbara credited her strategy for dealing with fear to a beloved uncle. As a young child, she used to seek safety by going into a room by herself when something scared her.
One day, when she was a little girl, there was summer shower that included some thunder, and Barbara went into the hall closet and hid her head behind the biggest coat she could find. Trying to coax her out, her uncle told Barbara she was missing something. He took her out into the gentle rain, and once assured the thunder was far away, she actually enjoyed herself. Her uncle told her, that's the best way to deal with fear. Just go out and face it. After a little bit your fears go away and you find you're having fun.

"Lots of times in my life I've wanted to hide in the closet, from problems, new experiences and new responsibilities," said Barbara. "But when I forced myself to come out and face them, I've found the thunder far away and the experience fun."

Barbara remained courageous to the end. She passed away on January 26, 2017 surrounded by family and loved ones. "We've all been so lucky to have her for so long," said her son Bill. "She was gracious and kind and silly and always fun to be with...a treasure as a friend and mother. We're all a little lost without her, but we have extraordinary stories and memories to take with us for the rest of our lives."

One of those memories comes from my dear friend Debbie Evans, who was extremely close to Barbara and spent a great deal of time at her home. Something she recently shared with fans sums up, for me at least, what Barbara was really like.

"Many a time I would answer the front door and find someone who had figured out her address. As I would politely try to tell them she wasn't accepting visitors, she would sweetly come up behind me and welcome them with a hug and a thank you. Sometimes a cup of coffee, sometimes a few roses from her beautiful rose garden. After they left, I would lecture her about talking to strangers. And she would correct me, and tell me they weren't strangers to her."

There's something special about knowing that the woman we admired for bringing so much joy into *our* lives viewed us as the people who brought so much joy into *her* life. It's comforting to realize that Barbara felt so close to us, and I hope after reading this book, you feel closer to her.

By the Same Author

How the real-life chemistry between Barbara Hale and Raymond Burr made a Perry/Della romance inevitable!

Also by Brian McFadden

Raymond Burr looks back on his days as America's favorite television lawyer!

By the Same Author

The story of two extraordinary stars who fought to change the way working women were portrayed on television!

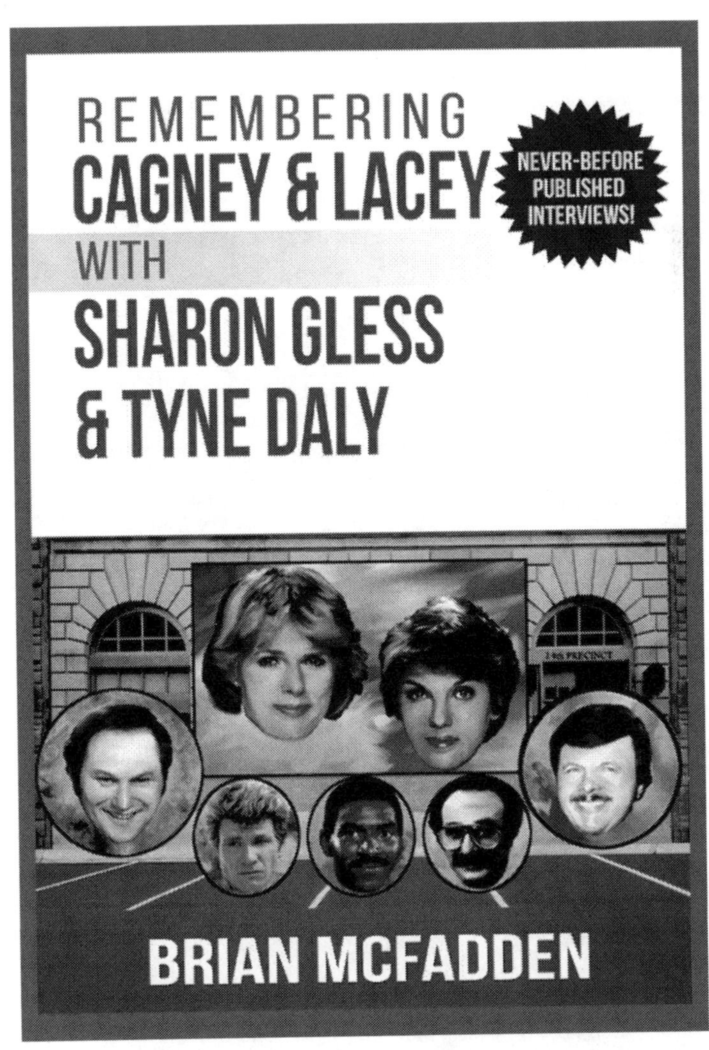

Also by Brian McFadden

The true story of the fearless young woman who overcame male-dominated Hollywood barriers to produce the original *Halloween, The Fog* and other cult classics, as well as award-winning film favorites like *The Fisher King*.....

ABOUT THE AUTHOR

Veteran broadcast journalist Brian McFadden has covered the entertainment industry for many years. Working for both United Press International and Wall Street Journal Radio, he also wrote for prominent movie and music magazines and was a news anchor on some of New York City's largest stations.

In addition to a series of popular books on television and motion pictures, McFadden is the author of the groundbreaking music works, "Rare Rhythm and Blues on Budget LPs" and "Rock Rarities for a Song – A Guide to Budget LPs that Saved the Roots of Rock 'N' Roll." The author and his wife live in the Somerset Hills of New Jersey.

The front cover artwork for this book is courtesy of Veronica Espinoza Paul. The back cover artwork is courtesy of Sonia Hill. Unless otherwise noted, all dates referred to are the release dates of the movies and shows mentioned, as opposed to the actual production dates. The illustrations in this reference/research work are used for historic and scholarly purposes under the "Fair Use Doctrine" of the US copyright law and are the property of the original copyright holders.